War, Baby

Kevin Mitchell was born in Blantyre, Malawi, in 1950 and, via Roscommon, Birmingham and Maitland, NSW, ended up at the *Observer* in 1990. He is the paper's chief sports writer. In 2000, the Sports Writers Association voted him their sports writer of the year, sports feature writer of the year and highly commended him in his specialist field, boxing.

WAR, BABY

The Glamour of Violence

KEVIN MITCHELL

YELLOW JERSEY PRESS
LONDON

Published by Yellow Jersey Press 2001

2 4 6 8 10 9 7 5 3

First published in Great Britain in 2001 by
Yellow Jersey Press
Random House, 20 Vauxhall Bridge Road,
London SW1V 2SA

Random House Australia (Pty) Limited
20 Alfred Street, Milsons Point, Sydney,
New South Wales 2061, Australia

Random House New Zealand Limited
18 Poland Road, Glenfield, Auckland 10, New Zealand

Random House (Pty) Limited
Endulini, 5A Jubilee Road, Parktown 2193, South Africa

The Random House Group Limited Reg. No. 954009
www.randomhouse.co.uk

Photographs reproduced by kind permission of Vanessa Winship, Teddy Blackburn, Dan Smith

A CIP catalogue record for this book
is available from the British Library

ISBN 0-224-06072-4

Papers used by Random House are natural, recyclable products made from
wood grown in sustainable forests; the manufacturing processes conform
to the environmental regulations of the country of origin

Typeset in Janson MT by SX Composing DTP, Rayleigh, Essex
Printed and bound in Great Britain by
Biddles Ltd, Guildford and Kings Lynn

CONTENTS

Dedicated to the young soldier who got in the ring with Sgt Joe Louis at Aldershot in the summer of '43. Thanks, Dad.

Gerald McClellan, lean and moody, in the King's Cross gym on his first visit to London, in November 1991. © Vanessa Winship.

Acknowledgements

This was always going to be the sort of book I didn't want my mother to read. Some of the language is a bit strong, you see. But it's the lingua franca of professional boxing. Rough and colourful, like a bad apple. As a steaming lump, it describes an ugly, intriguing story.

So thanks, among many others, to Vicious, Midnight, Stan, Stan's sister Margerie, the Black Battle Cat, Silas, Nightmare, the Iceman, Ted in LA, Al in Milwaukee and Hyacinthus Turnipseed – whoever and wherever you are, Junior.

Nigel Benn, who'd written his own book, talked candidly about his fight with Gerald McClellan. So did his estranged manager, Peter DeFreitas. And his estranged promoter, Ambrose Mendy.

Strange world, boxing.

Benn's last trainer, Kevin Sanders, talked for the first time about his friendship with McClellan – and the foreboding that gripped him in the moments before the fight. Dennie Mancini told me how a meeting with a blind man on the morning of the fight persuaded him Nigel was going to win.

In Freeport, Illinois, where Gerald grew up, early talk of a street named in his honour, or a statue, vanished with the passing of the pity. Some citizens, though, like Edgar Oppenheimer, Roger Kerr and Mat Marvin, haven't forgotten their town's best ever fighter. As well as Sunshine, of Sunshine Liquor. And the guys who said Sunshine was talking bullshine.

It's that sort of story. Gathered around the principal characters, a cast of comedians tried to 'put the record straight'. It wasn't easy sifting through their more bizarre claims.

Gerald's immediate family had a lot to say, especially his sister Lisa. She is a combative gatekeeper to the McClellan story, but I can only say that, whatever her arguments with others (and there were many), she was generous with her time once she reckoned I was worth trusting.

Brendan Ingle, who held the spit bucket in Gerald's corner, was his colourful self. So was Gary Newbon, who was at the microphone the night ITV were getting ready to pull the plug on big-time boxing.

Emanuel Steward, who'd split with Gerald some time before the fight, told me of an interesting discussion he had with Roy Jones Jr about Gerald.

Frank Warren, whose conversations have often started with 'I've got a bone to pick with you', told me some of what went on behind the scenes. His partner that night, Don King, normally a talker of Olympian skill, fell strangely silent. To other absent friends – those who didn't return the phone calls – don't say you didn't have a chance to tell your story.

As for the archives, the Showtime and ITV commentaries provided a contemporary account of the action uncluttered by retrospection, and are all the more honest for that. There's a chunk of reference from Bob Mee's scholarly and bloody read, *Bare Fists*, as well as a swag of other boxing books, a few films – and a poem.

Reports by my fight-writing colleagues before and after the fight gave a variety of perspectives on a complicated story.

David Milner and Rachel Cugnoni proved to be patient taskmasters for Yellow Jersey. And my comrades at the *Observer*, the oldest and best Sunday newspaper in the world, put up with a bit of angst too. Especially Victoria Barrett, who shovelled the manuscript through the appropriate machines.

Thanks to Vanessa Winship and Teddy Blackburn for some rare photographs, and to Maria Belen Orihuela for translating M. Alfred Asaro's views on the fight.

I wish Harry Mullan could have read this before I committed it to print. Not only could he have spotted the factual idiocies which the forensically meticulous will no doubt go hunting for, but, more importantly, it would just be nice to have the excellent old Irish rascal around still.

Thanks, mainly, though, to Gerald – even though you haven't the faintest idea who I am.

And to Fiona who, for her sins, does.

Stoke Newington, summer 2001.

x

Foreword

Putting this book to bed in the summer, I was as surprised as anyone when Joltin' Johnny Prescott, the deputy prime minister, punched a demonstrator who attacked him in Rhyl during the General Election. Or was I? The smart columnists told us we should be appalled. Maybe we weren't. A majority of the population – as polled by the *Sun*, the arbiter of all our baseness – said they admired Joltin' Johnny for reacting as many of us would have done. Or would like to have done. There was something going on out there that the smart columnists did not quite get . . .

I'd not long returned from Portland, Oregon, where I met a man called Chuck Palahniuk. He grew up the working-class son of Ukrainian parents, went to university and drifted into a boring job. After eight years of writing service manuals for a local freight company, Chuck snapped. He started fighting in bars around Portland. Over nothing, often. Liberated by violence, Chuck kept punching. He was hooked. Then, as his bruises grew in proportion to his lack of popularity, he stopped fighting and started writing. He wrote a book and called it *Fight Club*. Hollywood found out, made a movie of his book and Chuck got rich. He doesn't fight in bars any more. But he says he understands now.

Chuck reckons men fight because we have been robbed of our masculine heritage. We don't know how to hunt or fight or fix a car engine any more, he says. Our fathers are to blame too, for not telling us about it. Nothing puts us in touch with our real inner-male selves, apparently, like a punch in the nose or an oily tappet head.

While I was going some way down his road, I thought the theory simplistic.

Yet it is obvious that the book and the movie hit a chord. Message boards all over the Internet posted requests looking for real fight clubs. Mormon students in Utah brawled; kids in garages started punching each other out; unlicensed boxing mini-boomed; wrestling, the theatrical parody of fighting, outsold real boxing.

It seemed there might be a bit of Joltin' Johnny Prescott in all of us.

Which brings us to what this book is about: why we are fascinated by violence. For many people, that unspoken question never shouted so loud as at the London Arena, on 25 February 1995, the night Nigel Benn fought Gerald McClellan. I'm fifty and have watched boxing since I was very young, dabbled a bit as a gauche schoolboy and, as a journalist, have been ringside at thousands of contests for more than thirty years – but I have never seen a fight quite so fierce as the one between Benn and McClellan. Few of the other writers or the 12,000 or so customers there that night had either. There was a similar reaction among the television audience of thirteen million. McClellan ended up blind and severely disabled. Benn fought on but was never the same again.

It was a fight that went to the very heart of our secret.

Introduction

The handsome young American had attitude. And a serious girl jones. One way or another, his days and nights were interesting.

And he could fight. So he was coming over to London, he said, to beat up on the veteran Englishman who claimed he was the best fighting man in the world. The champion, in his thirties, was still a celebrity athlete, a fighter who had made his reputation in major contests, someone who commanded a substantial following beyond his own precinct. It was no surprise, therefore, that the boxing hardcore for months had talked of little else but his showdown with the dangerous young American. Somebody was going to get badly hurt in this one.

Come the day, English fans got beered up and made for the venue like an army on heat. By fight-time, they were expecting, almost willing, the worst. Few present would forget what they saw. One of the smart writers later called it 'the highpoint of brutality'. And, not for the first time, the abolitionists said it was surely a fight to end all arguments in the sport's favour.

An estimated 12,000 members of the fancy left Waterloo railway station for an unknown field that April dawn in 1860. The day John Heenan fought Tom Sayers. It was the first, and not the last, Fight of the Century, an eerie precursor to Benn versus McClellan.

The tickets cost three guineas and were stamped 'to nowhere', lending spice and symbolism to an illicit adventure. Polite society viewed prizefighting with hypocritical ambivalence, and the law deemed it an exercise in barbarism. But then, as now, the public face did not reflect the soul within. So the blood addicts headed for Farnborough on the Hampshire–Surrey border like thieves in the dark, talking in that knowing whisper familiar to all conspirators.

The nineteenth century, like those before it, was an age of uncomplicated physicality. Duelling by this time was illegal, of course – although that did not stop the prime minister, the Duke of Wellington, swapping stray pistol shots with Lord Winchelsea in Battersea Park one morning in 1829, in a dispute over Catholic emancipation. Also outlawed were bear- and bull-baiting. Cock fighting too – a sure recipe for popularity. And their adherents wondered how these awful obsessions were better or worse than the sanctioned upper-class indulgence of fox-hunting. Or, for that matter, warmongering.

But it was fights between men – and sometimes women – that attracted the crowds and the money. As far back as 1690, a French visitor to London observed, 'Anything that looks like fighting is delicious to an Englishman.' A fist fight was still the biggest draw outside public hangings (which went on until 1868) – especially against someone from the former colonies.

It was not surprising, then, that the silk and satin of Savile Row rubbed up against a rotten-toothed, Hogarthian scrum that morning without a whit of self-consciousness. The gore-hunters were in good company. William Makepeace Thackeray was there for *Vanity Fair*. Charles Dickens went too. Lord Palmerston wanted the result relayed to 10 Downing Street as soon as it was known. They'd all get their three guineas' worth.

In America, the hysteria over Sayers v Heenan was heightened by distance. George Templeton Strong wrote in his diaries on the looming war between the Union and the Confederacy that 'the fight totally absorbed men's attention ... the symbolic ring of combat eclipsed all interest in the painful realities of sectional conflict'.

George Wilkes's newspaper, *Spirit of the Times*, said:

> The ordinary objections to vulgar pugilism are waived in the real importance of this first-class struggle, and there is scarcely a mind that is amenable to the national pride which does not for once lay aside its prejudice against fighting in the hope to see the American champion win.

The fixture, for £200 a side, started at 7.29 a.m., the weak spring sun dressing the business in a sickly warmth. They say £100,000 was laid in bets. National fervour ensured Sayers was backed into favouritism at 3–1 on, even though he was significantly smaller at 5ft 8in and 10st 12lb. Heenan, 6ft 2in and a pound under fourteen stone, chose to fight downhill on the slope, with the sun at his back.

In the sixth round, it looked as if the punters had 'done their dough' when Sayers took a hefty knock on his right arm and felt the bone crack. Heenan, who'd broken the odd limb fixing votes around San Francisco, went for a quick conclusion as the Englishman's injured arm dangled redundantly by his side. But he couldn't finish his man. Round after round Sayers was floored, sometimes heavily, sometimes not. Each time he came up to the mark. Reduced to ramming his left fist into the American's face, he gained strength in adversity; all the while, Heenan's frustrations enveloped him.

In the thirty-seventh round Sayers found himself on the wrong end of negotiations. The American, struggling to stay upright while looking out for Sayers's jab through hideously purpled eyes, grabbed his man and started to strangle him on the ropes. As the constabulary advanced, the fans crowded into the ring to rescue their champion. The action resumed briefly but the interruption forced an unruly end. In the confusion that followed, the referee was unable or unwilling to render a judgement for the gamblers on the status of the fight. So a contest which had been anticipated as a defining moment in prizefighting history ended in a draw after two hours and twenty minutes. Just in time for a late breakfast.

When the gathering dispersed for their sausages and ale, the hum was about a memorable, if inconclusive, collision of wills. Bell's *Life in London*, the bible of the day for sporting types, declared it 'decidedly the very best championship fight we ever witnessed'. As well they might: the paper's editor was a co-promoter with Wilkes, whose newspaper *Spirit of the Times* had done so much to feed the fires beforehand in America.

As for which were the better fighting nation, Bell strained for objectivity: 'The only point that has been decided, and the only point in our opinion requiring decision, is that both England and America possess brave sons, and each country had reason to be proud of the champion she had selected.'

Heenan went briefly blind, sailed back to New York to receive the rapturous acclaim of 50,000 people in a New York park – and then slid into anonymous decline. His fans apparently deserted him when he refused to sign up for the Union against the South, so he returned to England to fight in Sussex in 1863 and was given a fearsome hiding by Tom King. Having his old adversary Sayers in his corner, in drink and confused, might not have helped John's cause.

Poor John returned to the embrace of Adois Dolores McCord, a poet and stage artiste whose showbiz name was Adele (sometimes Adah) Isaacs Mencken (or Menken). She was a Broadway star, known to one and all as Mrs John Heenan. Afterwards, however, Adois/Adele/Adah abandoned her milling paramour – for, among others, Mr Dickens.

A year after ineptly seconding the American against King, Sayers died of drink, aged thirty-nine. They say 10,000 mourners accompanied him to Highgate Cemetery, where the illiterate cobbler's son from Brighton surely found more peace than he ever did alive.

Adele died four years later in Paris, aged thirty-three, leaving behind some excruciating poetry, some of it dedicated to her bewildered ex-lover. Heenan fought and lost a couple more times and, in 1873, he headed home to California in search of clean air to fix his gasping shell of a body. He didn't make it. When they found him, dead and alone in a hotel room in Green River, Wyoming Territory, he was destitute, his lungs leaking blood like a cut pig. He was thirty-eight and a legend of sorts. But John Camel Heenan – acknowledged as the man who gave America's most notorious and glamorous sport its first inspiration – never won a proper fight in his life.

While not every fighter finished up like Heenan and Sayers, the best business was done at the scene of the worse damage. As the prize grew in proportion to the suffering, it would take some moral gymnastics to provide fighting with a legitimate place in society – and there was no shortage of ingenuity applied to the task.

About this time, coincidentally or not, serious thinkers had begun analysing man's darker nature.

A year before Sayers–Heenan, Charles Darwin published *On the*

Origin of Species. His assault on the comfortable verities of religion, and his challenging of the long-held notion that our rightful place was nearer to God than the devil, provoked lively salon debate. If Darwin were right, would we ever shed our base nature? Would we for ever be fighting in fields like animals, the strongest lasting longest before becoming dust like the rest? The row even caught the eye of laughing boy Nietzsche.

Germany's leading miserabilist said 'God is dead', announcing his disillusionment with spirituality. But he reckoned man should not merely turn away from a higher being but be prepared to control his own destiny. The Will to Power, he called it. George Bernard Shaw – one-time aspirant in the championships conducted by the Amateur Boxing Association, and later a friend of Gene Tunney – was among those who joined the chorus on Nietzsche's side. Fighting is what men did. And the better they did it, the better men they became.

Contrary to what Hitler would say later, Nietzsche's idea of the triumph of the will had little to do with race. Man overcame himself, suggesting he had control of the genes he had been given as well as the other forces in his life. It had nothing to do with biology, he said. It had nothing to do, either, with whether or not an Aryan was better than a black man, or an Englishman a better prizefighter than an American. Mostly, Nietzsche reckoned, it had nothing to do with God.

And Darwin, the failed medical student who fainted at the sight of blood, said it had everything to do with the survival of the fittest.

Maybe they should all have met at Farnborough. Maybe they did.

This, then, is the dark secret. The power of the punch. Proof that savagery outsells finesse is written in the history of the ring. Fighters came in many sizes and styles, but the great excitement generators are easily identified: there was Dempsey, the incomparable Welshman Jimmy Wilde, Jack 'Kid' Berg, Berg's palindrome Harry Greb (who boxed half-blind and trained on whores and whiskey), Ketchel, Mickey 'the Toy Bulldog' Walker. Since the war (the second one), we've had Zale and Graziano, 'Raging Bull'

La Motta, Marciano, Liston, Frazier, Ali, Chavez, Duran (except on the 'no mas' night he will not be allowed to forget), Holyfield, Bad Iron Mike ... and two young men who would discover when they met at the home of sanctioned violence how hooked they were on the essence of the fighting thing.

In its acceptable form, as living theatre, violence hypnotises its audience as it simultaneously gives its participants the dubious thrill of gambling with their own mortality for, sometimes, considerable sums of money.

If Benn and McClellan had fought at Farnborough, their fight would have been properly described as 'the highpoint of brutality'.

And, if you'd had the chance, you'd have paid your three guineas to be there, alongside Dickens and Thackeray and all the other allegedly innocent bystanders.

Seconds Out

'You go to war and you win this war, or you go to war and you die – you're not going to return. I'm not afraid of being in the ring, because it's my job.' – Gerald McClellan, 23 February 1995.

No pretence at civilisation could disguise the return to primal behaviour when Anglo-American hostilities came to town again, 135 years after Sayers–Heenan. There'd been memorable confrontations in the meantime, but this would be the last great tear-up for a while.

The mood was oppressive. Nasty too, and exciting. There was hardly a soul entering the London Arena who didn't expect something bad to happen.

McClellan, of Freeport, Illinois, had been installed to challenge Benn for his World Boxing Council twelve-stone title, and again an estimated 12,000 members of the fancy were on hand. As ever, they were raging fit to tear the place apart – and anyone who was there, or watched it at home, will be haunted by the grotesque magnificence that unfolded before them. For younger patrons, and some of the older ones too, it was the greatest fight they ever saw.

Barry McGuigan, who's been to the hard place and back, said beforehand, 'This is one of the most eagerly anticipated fights on both sides of the Atlantic for many, many years. It's going to be absolutely dynamite while it lasts.'

As when Sayers fought Heenan, the flags were run up and the money put down. However, unlike Farnborough, when the locals reckoned their champion would win, Benn was figured to be heading for a painful defeat. McClellan, a rangy six-foot hitter of scary elasticity, was physically more imposing than Benn, even though he was stepping out of the middleweight division for the first time; and, at twenty-seven years of age, he was nearly five years younger than the local champion. Not since Joe Louis did anyone own a better knockout percentage in title fights. Even though McClellan weighed in at a surprisingly light 11st 11lb, three pounds under the limit, not a single serious observer gave Benn a chance. The only voice in his favour came from the theatrical racing commentator John McCririck, a judgement possibly inspired by the urge to be noticed as by any sensible examination of the evidence. Aside from McCririck, Nigel Benn's backers were purblind patriots, friends and the hired help. There has been much speculation about who the co-promoters were backing; Frank Warren, who put the fight on with Don King, says he had Benn to win at 5–2. King? As ever, he came to town waving his Stars and Stripes – although I was to learn later his allegiance wasn't as straightforward as it looked.

Nigel couldn't buy a friend in the papers. *The Times* predicted it would be all over for Benn by the sixth; the *Mirror* thought he might reach the fifth; the *Express*, the *Star* and the *Sun* went for the guest from Illinois in three; the *Independent* and the *Mail* thought he'd do it in two; and the *Guardian*'s widely respected John Rodda reckoned McClellan would finish it inside a round. I thought Benn would go out gloriously in a five-round war. The visiting American writers voted the party line.

Benn read the headlines and was unimpressed by the lack of support. Although a proud, London-born black Briton, he was not so much fighting now for his country, his turf or the colour of his skin, but for himself. He was McClellan's Nietzschean nightmare. He would overcome.

Benn was used to standing up for himself. There are two quick ways out of London's East End: thieving and boxing. Some took no chances and tried both. Certainly Nigel dabbled in juvenile delinquency, and there were plenty of like-minded citizens there that night. They brought with them a powerful aura of trouble. These were the boys hanging on to the fag-end of football hooliganism's extended reign. This was a no-nonsense, unsubtle hard-man's fight.

Hard men such as Dave Courtney and Tony Tucker.

Courtney described Benn as 'one of my best pals' and liked to be known in London's gangland as the Enforcer. His *nom de guerre* stemmed from his work as a debt collector. A man who knew where to get a gun quickly, he arranged the security at Ronnie Kray's funeral. Courtney carried a solid-gold knuckleduster with diamond-studded ridges, monogrammed 'D.C.', and once stuck a fork in the face of an adversary who knocked on his door looking for a showdown. Legend has it, and so does he, that he was the inspiration for Vinnie Jones's character in the movie *Lock, Stock & Two Smoking Barrels*. He's made a fair (and sometimes legal) living out of his violent life – he's written a book about it, as well as fronting a TV documentary about violence. And he liked nothing better than hanging around Nigel.

Once, in Tenerife, they were out running when Benn was training for a fight. A dozen or so members of the 18–30 brigade confronted them and a small brawl ensued. Courtney later boasted how well he had performed alongside the world champion.

Tucker, another face with a good ringside view that night, had been a familiar figure at big-time boxing for years, often acting as Nigel's bodyguard. Later in the year, Tucker and two associates were shotgunned to hell while sitting in a car at the end of an Essex country lane, a drugs war brought to a full stop. Or, more likely, a comma.

Nigel has always been candid about his roots. Many of his old friends get a namecheck in his autobiography, and most of those who were still at large were at the London Arena. Benn had done his share of petty thieving at school, bullying classmates for their lunch money, rucking in the street and generally getting rid of any energy he had left over after an unusually enthusiastic study of sex. He admits he was once tempted to take part in robbing a security van of £500,000, but says, 'I bottled out. I decided then that I wanted to make an honest living.'

So he chose boxing.

And there they all were. The 'security operatives', hooligans, hangers-on, voyeurs of every description. 'Enger-lund! Enger-lund!' Around the hall orange shirts, lemon shirts, red shirts, green shirts, blue shirts, worn outside slacks, housed rumbling bellies, and crazied-up eyes told their own story. This was the winter uniform of the slightly mad. Pumped on pills and lager, the aficionados of violence couldn't wait for the off. So they started their own entertainment. A scuffle broke out in the cheap seats but not many of the participants wanted to risk damage to their smart threads or, worse, ejection. It calmed down soon enough.

They'd come from every corner of the East End, and beyond, the Essex hinterland their parents had made their own. 'Sarf', as well. It seemed like every pissed bad-hat for a hundred miles had congregated to 'watch some other fucker fight for a change'. And two 'black geezers' at that. There is little racial tension at the business end of boxing – in the gym or the ring – but you still get the intellectuals with old prejudices paying at the gate. Still, when Benn was fighting, they saw no colour. He won respect across the board. He'd earned the right to rule as the People's Champion. Nobody excited a boxing crowd like the Dark Destroyer. And, tonight, he was British. For half an hour or so, the power of his fighting drowned out straight-up racial bigotry. But not xenophobia.

Those who paid most got closest. They dressed expensively and moved with assurance among the B-list celebs. And, wherever they sat, all of them, rich and near-skint, were quick to identify a stranger. 'Outsiders' felt intimidated. The American TV crew, led by Showtime's Ferdie Pacheco, said only a fight in Mexico could generate the same sense of unease as they felt at ringside in London that night. This wasn't simple patriotism – it was tribal pride curdling into unmistakable anti-Americanism. Just like Farnborough.

It was clear that this was a big night because a lot of people had paid good money to attend a fight they could have watched live and, more importantly, free on television at home. It would be the last-but-one major terrestrial TV fight of the century. Naseem Hamed fought and won spectacularly in Scotland on ITV the following Saturday. But Benn–McClellan was the one you had to be at. Naz broke training to be there in the front row. Frank Bruno, soon to get ready for Oliver McCall, sat (or mostly stood) nearby. Press accreditation was tight and all the big-hitters from the American Fight Writers fraternity were there.

McClellan was only mildly concerned about these details. He had to get down to business. Benn was hard but McClellan reckoned he was harder. He'd think nothing of betting $10,000 on a pit-bull fight in a side street in Detroit, and he gambled with the confidence of someone who knew where he could get more if he needed it. The price wasn't attractive this time though; he'd been 2–1 on all week, firming to 4–1 on, then easing to 5–2 on by Saturday. You could back Benn at 40–1 in any one of the twelve rounds. There weren't many takers.

Both fighters came to the ring wound up to an unbearable point of intensity. Responding to the promotional demands to hype that which needed no hyping, McClellan issued his chilling declaration of war two days before the fight. Now those words were swimming inside his head. They wouldn't go away.

'You go to war … you win … you die – you're not going to return … I'm not afraid … it's my job … not going to return … you win … you die … my job … not afraid … not going to return … my job.' These were the thoughts that would follow him into the ring. And, when it was over, all the way back to Freeport. Years later, Benn would look back on the fight. 'To me it was just work,' he said.

Gerald had sounded detached and cold on the Thursday. In his rolling drawl he was putting down a pre-fight marker. The Fight Writers had heard it too often, though. Regulation American baloney. But it made a headline. King knew that. He was in his big-time showbiz mode and picked up on the theme. 'This is war, baby! Heh, heh!'

With about half an hour to go, Benn was itching to get it on. He had plenty of incentive, not least the £700,000 (including VAT) he was guaranteed. He needed the money. The taxman was getting impatient. For McClellan, finances were less complicated. And smaller. When it was done, when the bills and the tax and the expenses and the rest had been calculated, Gerald would end up with less than $63,000. Not much when you consider the money that was being generated by him and his opponent. Admission prices had risen somewhat since Sayers–Heenan, and, with the money from ITV and the American boxing outlet, Showtime, the pot was substantial. This was no low-rent Saturday night street fight. Although it came close.

As well as the sums on offer, each of them had the prospect of meeting the unbeaten Roy Jones for more money than they'd ever earned before. McClellan reckoned that match-up was his: he'd beaten Jones as an amateur (about the same time he beat the future world heavyweight champion Michael Moorer), and he was getting better by the fight. Neither boxer was to know that Jones had no intention of risking his reputation against anyone remotely dangerous, that he would pad out his career against a succession of second-rate opponents while somehow convincing his media admirers he was the best pound-for-pound operator in the business.

In the moments before they went to the ring, Nigel had worked himself into a state, while Gerald was struck by a cold, sense-sapping apprehension. Cus D'Amato, who shaped the young Tyson, urged fighters to use this fear. And now, with the fight about to start, Gerald had to turn himself into Superman. 'Walking from the locker room to the ring is the scariest feeling I ever had in my life,' he said. 'It's like I have butterflies, my heart's beating hard, I'm already sweating, my hands are wet, it's just a real scary feeling.'

Then into McClellan's dressing room walked a familiar face. Kevin Sanders, Nigel's new trainer, had known Gerald since the Freeport boxer was an amateur and Sanders was on his learning tour of United States gyms. He was in the other corner when McClellan lost to a good amateur called Ray McElroy in the final of the 1988 Golden Gloves.

'Hey, Kevin! What you doin' here?'

'I'm with Nigel. I'm in his corner tonight.'

Sanders, a late replacement for Jimmy Tibbs, who'd asked for and not received £40,000, had come to inspect the wrapping of Gerald's hands, as is boxing's custom. It is a gesture of fair play, designed to guard against the sort of trickery Jack Dempsey is said to have pulled on poor old Jess Willard, on the afternoon he knocked the big man out with loaded gloves. Kevin didn't reckon on finding any underhand activity, it was just a formality.

But, as he was walking back to Nigel's dressing room, Sanders thought about what he'd just seen: Gerald was wrapping his own hands. Fighters will do this in the gym, but just before a contest? It's not only difficult, it's pretty much impossible to do properly. The last time Sanders had seen a boxer wrap his own hands before a fight, that fighter, Robert Wangila, had died. 'He was a good friend,' Sanders had said later. 'I was with him to the end.'

A boxer's hands are bomb sites, bumpy with hillocks of crunched-up gristle and bone. Much of the damage is inflicted on the back of the fist and near the wrist. That's where bones break if the wrapping isn't sound. I've seen it done expertly, trainers dragging the bandage tightly and precisely across the base of the wrist, securing the middle part of the thumb to bring balance to the hand, bulking up over the outside knuckles to level off the hitting area at the top of the fist, which relieves pressure on the two more prominent knuckles, then bringing the bandage around and under to form a comfortable ball in the palm of the hand. This is the Manny Steward method, copied by a lot of American and British trainers. What it puts on the end of a boxer's arm is a wrecking ball. As Glenn McCrory, the former world cruiserweight champion, put it to me once, wrap your fists up the right way and you can punch through a wall. Get it wrong and you're hitting with candyfloss.

Gerald had arrived in London without Steward or Willie Brown, his regular trainer and the man who latterly had been wrapping his hands. Brown had learnt his boxing arts with Steward at the Kronk academy in Detroit and was loyal to him, having trained other Steward fighters over several years. Not long after McClellan split with Steward, Willie became unavailable. He told Gerald he was leaving the game, getting married. Gerald didn't believe him.

Steward reckoned later that everything was wrong about McClellan's preparation for the fight. Why, for instance, had McClellan come in three pounds under the twelve-stone limit? He'd moved up from middleweight after complaining he couldn't make that limit any more, and here he was at 11st 11lb. It looked like the challenger had miscalculated his fine-tuning – 'nosedived at the weight', as Sanders put it. Steward used to do McClellan's cooking for him before a fight, to ensure his diet was sound and his weight loss steady. Then they fell out.

That was a year ago now. Gerald owed him and his manager of record, John Davimos, $119,000. On fight night, therefore, the

Kronk guru was sitting in front of the television back home in the States, and so, Gerald picked up the gauze and wrapped his hands. He would overcome.

He looked around the room. There stood his chief second Stan Johnson, Gerald's cousin Donnie Penelton, the cuts man Ralph Citro and a new boy – Hyacinthus Turnipseed, or Junior, as the McClellans knew him. Neither Stan nor Donnie – alongside Citro and Brendan Ingle, who was holding the spit bucket for £20 and a ringside seat that night – knew Mr Turnipseed from a buttered parsnip. 'But, hey,' said Donnie, 'Gerald's the champ. He have who he damn well want.' Taking pictures – some of them in this book – was Vanessa Winship, a British photographer who had met Gerald on his first visit to London and was fascinated by boxing. Her normal beat was war.

Sanders couldn't dwell on Gerald, or Robert Wangila. If McClellan was going in with candyfloss rather than wrecking balls, Benn might get through the inevitable early onslaught. And Sanders knew more about McClellan than any of the experts who'd made him a certainty. 'I knew that Gerald hardly ever sucked in any water [while boiling down before a fight] because of his weight problems. And, he never went beyond eight rounds because he banged everybody out. Also, Gerald was a very straight puncher, a tremendously straight, long-arm puncher. So I had a game plan even before we went to camp because I'd seen Gerald so regularly.'

He would get Benn to weave in close, à la Tyson, get under McClellan's spear-like jabs and crosses, throw rights over the top, then disengage and come again, jabbing for range and hooking around McClellan's guard. It was a simple, sensible strategy. Nigel, never a fancy boxer, had another trick. He had become adept at using the ropes as a launching pad. He would crouch and sway, inviting a downward retaliation, then spring upwards with hooks. He refined the technique when in Miami with the expatriate London boxing personality, Vic Andreetti. It was a high-risk, high-return style of fighting. And dramatic.

Sanders was confident and so was Benn. The underdog had as much faith in himself as the favourite did, so it was a proper contest, a rarity in elite professional boxing. Neither fighter thought

London Arena, 1995. McClellan wraps his own hands, watched by a supervisor, his chief second, Stan Johnson, and Benn's trainer, Kevin Saunders. © Vanessa Winship.

about being badly injured, even if the chances of that happening were significant. McGuigan once said, 'Ninety-nine per cent of boxers take up the sport because they want to feel respected. The worry of performing badly and being made to look foolish is greater than the worry of getting hurt.'

These were two proud artists of pain, each with the capacity to humiliate and inflict serious injury. At ringside, the pre-fight rituals continued. We settled in, with statistics at hand and preconceptions ready to be exploded. But, as the mob murmured, there was an unusual quiet about the press area, where normally banter and gossip fly like chicken feathers. I felt my heart beating. I looked over at Harry Mullan, one of our best. He was quiet too. All around were the seasoned and the cynical. Nobody was saying much. Hugh McIlvanney, Colin Hart. These were writers who'd seen most of the major ring action of the past quarter of a century. Not one of them owned a palm that wasn't sweating.

The fighters and their seconds walked grimly to the ring, McClellan first. Benn had called on the services of Dennie Mancini, one of the best cuts men in boxing, and a sound old head in a crisis. On his way to the venue that sunny morning, he'd met a blind man in the street, an old soldier and friend of his brother's. Dennie had stopped to say hello, and felt good about that. The old boy had smiled, grateful for a small kindness. 'I knew then,' Mancini recalled, 'that this was going to be a special fight. And I knew then that Nigel would win.'

Also with Benn was his manager, Peter DeFreitas, who knew something about Nigel that even the boxer himself did not know at the time.

Up on the TV gantry, Jim Rosenthal observed, 'Boxing can make a complete idiot of anyone who's brave enough to make a prediction, but you can be absolutely sure we're in for something very special in the next hour.'

Not such an idiot after all, Jim.

Alfred Asaro, a dandy-looking Parisian with thoroughly combed hair, stands in one of the two neutral corners. He would look more at home in a bistro back on the Champs Élysées, armed with nothing more threatening than an over-priced menu. As it is M. Asaro is a fully qualified and experienced referee and has been put in charge of a world title fight between two dangerous fighters, neither of whom understands a single word of French. Whoops, M. Asaro doesn't speak English either. But he was the man selected for the job. The procedure for choosing referees is that the World Boxing Council whose championship is being contested, selects a referee from a panel which, more or less, works on rotation. It was Asaro's turn. They announced his selection just before the fight. Afterwards, a lot of people would say it was a seriously poor choice.

He calls them together. Waves his hands about. A babble of words follow. In fractured English. Neither fighter listens. They miss nothing of conse-quence. 'I please . . . Break? Right there . . . Like head? [Touching his fore-head.] Head? Stop, stop . . . OK?' He sounds like Inspector Clouseau. Except it's not funny.

The G-Man's slim body glistens with sweat, part nerves, part fitness-heat. The noise slices his head. Out beyond the lights, the fans are beyond frenzy-point.

'Hey, Donnie! Ya hear me? I knock this guy out, these people ain't gonna tear into me, are they?'

'Listen, Gerald, you just go out there and knock him out. But Gerald?'

'Yeah?'

'Don't try to run back to the damn locker room after . . . We gonna git under the ring, coz they gonna try and tear the fuckin' place up!'

'Stan! Mouthpiece! Let's get this motherfucker outta here . . . Don't worry, Donnie, we'll be back in Freeport, no time . . . Let's go . . .'

2

Round One, Part Two   *Good Kid, Bad Kid*

McClellan goes to work. Rips to the body, head, up and down. In his own head, he writes the fight.

'This be over soon ... Want to clinch, eh? You better stay in close man, coz that the only place you safe. Back off, you sonofabitch! Taste some of this! And this! Yeah, go on back to the ropes muhfuh! You goin' home real soon! I got your number, man!'

The fight is a little over half a minute old. Benn's neck snaps back violently. Gerald's punches flow, free and fast. All Nigel can see are lights and leather. His arms flap uselessly and his eyes roll. His mouth lolls open and the spinning ring is a strange, familiar home of disaster. Benn falls against the ropes. They sag under his dead weight and cradle him as more vicious blows invade his brain and body.

Benn topples out through the ropes. McClellan smells victory.

'Bang! Over you go and bye-bye, motherfucker! Through them ropes, Mr Big Benn. We finished with you! . . .'

Alfred Asaro mores into the gap left by Benn, hand raised.

'Start countin', referee! Start fuckin' countin' on this muhfuh! . . . This be easier than I ever thought it gonna be . . . Man, I'm up there now! I'll be talkin' to you in just a second, Ferdie! Then we goin' after Roy Jones. Beat him again. Best in the whole damn world, then. Rich too. That motherfucker King better get me that damn fight. Don't want no more damn dumb contracts neither. This my time . . . Stan and Donnie and me, we're on toppa this . . . We come a long way, and we're goin' home with this motherfuckin' belt . . . Look at that damn Destroyer man on his ass . . .

'Is this motherfuckin' referee ever gonna finish this motherfuckin' count?'

While McClellan was waiting for the kill to be officially stamped and sealed, Benn was rearranging his brain. They were thirty-five seconds into the fight and he found himself flat-backed in the enemy corner. Crises don't come much starker. By the time he'd scrambled back through the ropes – 'like a drunk getting through a half-open window', as the *Telegraph*'s Paul Hayward memorably described it – the count had reached thirteen. But, to the amazement of many, he was still in the fight – and he didn't get upright without a little help.

'When he fell right across our monitors,' ITV's Gary Newbon recalls, 'I thought, "Bloody hell, it's all over." And then I pushed him back towards the ring, before I realised what I'd done. I looked around, but I didn't think anybody had spotted it.'

Technically, then, it could have been over, right there. Reg Gutteridge, Newbon's colleague sitting at another microphone maybe twelve feet away, saw the assist, but not the assistant, and informed the viewers, 'They've parked the rules at the gate tonight.'

Many at the ringside thought the referee's count slow. It was. Peter DeFreitas, however, said they were 'talking crap'. He said Nigel hit the apron and, consequently, had fifteen seconds to get back in the ring, not just the ten given for a regulation count. The board say it's actually twenty seconds. I've timed it on video: after Benn's thirteen-second absence from the fray, Asaro kept McClellan off him for a further five seconds. Jim Watt, at the ITV microphone, was unimpressed: 'Again the referee's being a little bit kind to Benn here. It's as if he's trying to help him survive this round.'

Whatever the post-fight arguments over times and rules, this was just another imponderable. Like the G-Man's fists. If McClellan, one of boxing's all-time hardest-hitting middleweights, had brought Steward or Brown with him to wrap his hands for his first fight at twelve stone, the blows he landed on Benn in that first round almost certainly would have been the definitive, fight-finishing ones. Never mind thirteen seconds, Benn might have been out for a minute or more.

McClellan was nursing a right hand that had both hurt and been hurt before. It had taken nearly a year to heal. He might not have held back in the initial blows, but how much 'English', how much brain-numbing, twisting torque, could he apply along that muscled right arm, down through toughened wrists and into his gloved hammer? And, if he did it once, could he do it three, four, five times in succession and not fear a break? While fighters are used to punching through pain, the subconscious reluctance to save something for later is strong – especially among thinking fighters, and Gerald was one of those. If Benn was getting up, he'd get him sooner or later.

Nigel was lucky to have a 'later' to contemplate. What he had to do now was stand up and claw his way back into a nightmare. He'd done it before – but this was by some way his most awesome challenge.

Just as Heenan, bigger and stronger, could not find the trick to subdue Sayers, so McClellan discovered that Benn would not go quietly. As Gerald waited to resume his attack, he grabbed a look at his corner. He was some character, that Stan . . .

Stan Johnson stretched out on a blanket near the lake with his girl-friend by his side and their young daughter nearby. Times weren't bad. Not as bad as they could be, had been, would be. Johnson was in the 'baahxin bizness'. That meant aggravation. But right now, a summer's day in the late seventies, the sun over Milwaukee felt good. This was the city where they chose to set *Happy Days*, television's depiction of fifties milk-bar America. Anyone from the north side, where the best crack houses and boxing gyms are, found it funny that their city was the TV home to Howard, Ralph, Pottsy and the Fonz. Not a life Stan knew. But, for a few minutes, it was sunshine time. Stan had reason to believe life might be all right for a while.

He closed his eyes and tried some more dreaming. All boxers dream. Some have nightmares. Stan was never going to be anyone's nightmare. Not in the ring, anyway. On 20 August 1970, he'd taken a gun and robbed a bank. He did five out of eight years. When he came out, he went straight. Usually it was straight into a left hook.

Stan had his first recorded paid fight in 1981, a couple of weeks after his thirtieth birthday, and was stopped in two rounds by Alfonso Ratliff, once a decent fighter, later a Frank Bruno sacrifice. Stan's career, if that is not too grand a description, went from awful to unbelievably bad. What highlights there were thereafter were submerged in a sea of defeats. He managed three wins – all stoppages – in thirty-nine contests over nineteen years. The rest of the time he mostly saw a man in a bow tie standing over him, counting.

Stan was not there to win. He was there to absorb, to go down, to go home. In twenty-six assignments he went home very early – like after a round. Occasionally he made it to the second, third or even the fourth before being stopped – and twice, over six and eight rounds, he actually went the distance. His finest hour – or eighteen minutes – was losing over six to Stefan Tangstad, the European heavyweight champion, and one-time world-title challenger. Stan got in the shape of his life for that one, coming in at a lightest ever 185 pounds, and might even have been trying to win it.

In 1987, Illinois records showed 'retired permanently/very poor'. But Stan kept boxing: in Minnesota, Virginia, Oklahoma, Kentucky ... anywhere they'd have him. The courts had tried to ground Stan by taking his passport away. Didn't work. He went touring, losing in some exotic rings, Germany, France, Brazil, big towns, small towns, against big and small names. And nearly always he went home with an 'L' against his name.

In 1998, he got a licence in Indiana, a state where they'd let your mother fight if you could find an opponent. That's where Stan Johnson had his last recorded fight, in March 2000. He weight 272 pounds and was knocked out in his favourite round – the first – by someone called Allan Smith. Even Indiana suspended him for thirty days. I would not bet that this was his last fight, even at the age of forty-nine. He doesn't know anything but the 'baahxin' business'.

Stan got shuffled in the pack.

'Damn! What the fuck that damn noise?'

Stan rouses from his dreaming to see a couple of stick-thin teenagers throwing rocks up at a tree, not far from where his four-year-old daughter was walking. He can tell the taller of the two is the sort of kid who won't stay in kidsville long. Stan springs up, grabs him and shouts in his face. 'Hey, man! You just see a little girl over there? You throwin' those fucking rocks up in that tree, whatever, one o' those rocks hit my little daughter on the head, I snatch your fuckin' heart outta you body and take a bite outta it!'

'These ain't rocks, mister,' Gerald McClellan says. 'These just apples.'

'Heh, yeah, they's just fuckin' green apples! Yeah, that's OK. So stop throwin' 'em any-fuckin'-way.'

Stan gave Gerald a 'push along his throat', as he described it years later, picked up his daughter and went back to his blanket.

It might have ended there, a spat between the pissed-off, ex-con boxer and the too-smart kid. But Gerald and Stan would see each other again.

Gerald had already tried a bit of boxing. Back in Freeport when Gerald was eight, his father Emmite had given him and his brother Anthony, known as Todd, a pair of boxing gloves for Christmas.

Gerald and Todd loved it, Todd more so at first. Their mother, Genola, wasn't keen on her boys doing what she called 'all of that fighting stuff'. But Emmite said different.

Emmite, only a little older than Stan, had been in the army and regarded himself as a hard man. He worked at the Chrysler plant in Belvidere when he came out of the service. There were several members of the Emmite McClellan clan, most of them around the same age. There's Sandra, who's the oldest, mid-thirties as I write; Anthony, Vincent, Emmite Jr; Lisa and Stacey; they have two other brothers, Andre and Mike, in Mississippi, one's the same age as Gerald and one's the same age as Stacey. 'Big family, yeah,' says Lisa. 'Four of them are just my half-brothers.'

Emmite said once of the family boxing programme, 'I started them going tough and rough. I had them cross-country running when Gerald was five. They'd run three or four miles a day. I'd run with them. Still run three or four miles a day.'

He'd get Gerald and Todd up at five in the morning, stick the gloves on them, mark out a ring on the sidewalk and make them spar under the street lights. 'Todd was a little older and stronger, but it was pretty much tit for tat,' Emmite told the *Freeport Journal-Standard*. 'Even when Gerald was little, I don't think anybody on the block could whup him. He was just gifted.'

Gerald knew Todd was the tough guy, 'but I was the more intelligent boxer. I used my head more. He'd try to do it with brute strength. That don't get it done all the time. If you weighed it out between skill and power, I think skill would win out.'

Emmite Sr's brother, Cornelius, would help in the early days. Cornelius boxed professionally, won twelve times and lost once. Not against name opposition, but he was handy. The family moved to Erie, Pennsylvania, when Gerald was eleven or twelve, Emmite saying they needed a change. He started up as a car mechanic there. Gerald liked Erie. This is where he met Hyacinthus Turnipseed. Or Junior, as some knew him.

Then Gerald came home from school one day and 'everything was packed up on the U-haul. Everybody was leaving.' This time, the move was for Gerald.

Emmite told his local newspaper that Milwaukee, where he'd been born, was the sort of town with tough gyms, the sort of places that would harden Gerald up, make him a champion. He thought he had a better crack at it than Todd, more coordinated. But Gerald wasn't that keen. 'He forced me to do it. My father would make me run, make me do push-ups, make me fight my brother and make me be at the gym on time every day. It just became a habit after a while.'

The way Emmite told it, it was his determination that drove Gerald. Probably was. As he told the local paper, Gerald was his 'number one priority'. They'd drive as far as South Carolina, sleep in the car. Emmite would close down his business and make sure his little star got all the good boxing there was. 'The other kids didn't like it much,' Emmite admitted.

It was about this time that Stan was nurturing talent around north Milwaukee and doing not bad. 'So,' remembers Stan, 'Gerald's father comes in the gym one day and he says, "I heard you the boxin' coach, I want you to train my son, his name Gerald." And Gerald steps in, looked at me and, hey, it's the kid in the park. And he just definitely did not like me, and he told his father, he wasn't fightin' for me – "Fuck that!" '

Gerald was at another gym at the time. He'd lost to a hotshot there called Anthony 'Nightmare' Pearson. Emmite wanted to move, to let his kid develop. Stan says his gym was bigger, that he had seven Wisconsin Golden Gloves champions. That meant he was coach of the Golden Gloves team, virtually. So Gerald, who was on his way up, even then, would come under his tutelage, whatever. It was a tough school. Emmite was right: Milwaukee was a good place for a champion in the making.

Aside from Stan, Gerald's other major influence was Al Moreland. They couldn't have been more different in their approach to boxing and all it had to offer. Al was as much a saver of souls as a boxing trainer. He's dabbled in pro boxing, but he reckons it wrecks lives. The amateurs, if it were run properly – 'which it definitely is not' – provides young boxers with something else, says Al. If he's got twenty kids working in the gym, he says, and there's a burglary down the block, he can show the cops twenty kids that didn't do it.

There were a lot of good amateurs with Moreland, among them Tyrone Trice, who boxed in world-class company, and Bruce Finch, who fought Sugar Ray Leonard. He also trained Dangerous Don Lee, who fought Tony Sibson and was bamboozled by Herol Graham. Al is in his sixties, been in boxing around Milwaukee for about half a century. One of the better products in his School for the Barely Redeemable was Gerald.

Even then, most fight people who'd seen him recognised that Gerald was special, and everyone around him wanted him to do well. 'Gerald was a nice kid,' Moreland recalled. 'He had good punchin' power, kept his range, good outside puncher and devastatin' body puncher. But, when he got someone in trouble in the ring, he was kinda vicious. As a person, Gerald was a nice guy ... but, you know, as any amateur start makin' money – anybody, as far as that goes – you kinda watch your step a little more. He wasn't so much flamboyant ... you wouldn't even call him cocky; he was just really sure of himself. Quiet, but real confident of himself.'

Under the varied tutelage of Al and Stan, Gerald blossomed like a tough rose. Between 1984 and 1987 he was Wisconsin Golden Gloves champion, four in a row. That's the sort of form that gets the professionals interested. Sugar Ray Leonard, who trawled the amateurs for prospects, kept an eye on Gerald. Emmite's dream looked like it was taking shape. With Gerald, anyway. Todd won a state Golden Gloves tournament and gave up boxing. Joined a gang. Found drugs. Excitement. Then prison. Lisa said he dropped out when he was drawn against Gerald in the Golden Gloves and he didn't have the stomach to face his brother in the ring.

According to the *Freeport Journal-Standard*, Gerald, meanwhile, stuck firm, listened to his dad. And to Al. As well as the guy in the park. 'I was always quiet,' he said. 'Outside of going to school and the gym, I never did much. Todd was the one. I was too headstrong for all that foolishness. I think it came from my father and from me just knowing better.'

But Gerald knew which side of the tracks was labelled 'wrong'. He liked the dark side best. Stan Johnson, no angel, understood that. Things started to go wrong for Gerald at school. He'd already lost a year and dropped down into his younger sister Lisa's class. And then he didn't bother to pick up his diploma. His mother didn't like it but she recognised that fighting was 'what he wanted to do'.

Moreland was on Genola's side. 'Instead of young boxers going into the professional ranks,' he said, 'my thing has always been to get them a job, get them to go to school and try and get somethin' to fall back on, because if you get caught inside the ropes it could be the last time. That's it. Goodbye, for ever. I like to get a kid off the street and make a viable citizen of him. I got a lot of them out of jail, got a lot of 'em out of different bad situations.'

Stan was on the other side of the track from Al – the same side as Gerald. He'd headed for the pros as soon as he could. He would tell Gerald to stay amateur only as long as it got him ready to earn money.

So Gerald and Stan hitched up together. Gerald made the State team without fuss, and Stan was in his corner for the nationals. Things were going fine. His only real rival, 'Nightmare' Pearson, had been swallowed up by the street, along with Todd. Nightmare had been ranked as a pro. And to make a long story short, says Stan, he ended up inside. In prison, with twenty-seven wins and one loss. Nightmare's out and fighting again. But that was, like, the last time I spoke to Stan.

Al and Gerald lost touch. He knew he was never going to stop Gerald from turning pro. He knew Gerald was on Stan's wavelength, not his. When he heard about Gerald's condition, they hadn't spoken for years. He was saddened by the news but life moves on. Besides, some of the places Gerald went were not exactly Al's territory. Stan, though, will have Gerald inside his head for the rest of his life. And what you can't dispute is that Stan Johnson was there at the beginning and he was there at the end.

'Goddam! He's still there. The motherfuckin' Destroyer Man still there. You want some more, man? Got it. I'm ready to go home. Damn this fuckin' referee. Get outta the way, man, I'm tryin' to work. And Nigel just hangin' on . . . How you feelin', Benn? Your head sore enough? Hey, you still swingin', eh? Damn, can't get the range here. That's better. Shoot the right, left to the liver . . . He's soaking this up now, he's strugglin' . . . gotta get him outta here . . . I know this muhfuh can punch, but he can't have much left now . . . Fuck, what was that? Damn, where my legs go? Gotta get my breath back. Gonna have to finish this next round . . . gotta get him out . . . gotta get him out . . . Shit, what was that? This is my fight, my time . . . Damn! the bell gone.'

Gerald slumps on his stool and sucks in water. He reckons the count is long. Stan and Donnie nod. They'd get him next round.

Across the ring, Mancini is cleaning up a cut under Nigel's right eye. They ought to be worried. DeFreitas thinks to himself, 'God, he looks like he's been run over by a fuckin' bus. Should we pull him out?'

Sanders is worried too. But he's got faith in Benn. And he knows McClellan will not like it if there is no early finish. They had to go on. They had to trust their man to ride this out.

But it is the old hand, Mancini, who puts it in words of fewest syllables. No time for niceties. This is Dennie's moment, his gift to Nigel.

'Nigel! Nigel! Listen to me! You were brilliant! The bollocks! He's finished, the other guy. Now you've got to go out there and do to him what he done to you! I mean it. This is kill or be killed!'

'Right, Dennie . . . Fuckin' right!'

3

Round Two   *Essex: Man and Boy*

Warmed-up, nerves gone, they go to it. From here on, it is an uncomplicated, savage row. Nothing to do with titles, money, the crowd. No movie could tell this story. The fighters hear, see, smell nothing but the Fight. There is no world outside their twenty-foot by twenty-foot ring. The press conferences, TV, all the stories had gone before. Arguments with trainers and managers do not crowd their thoughts. No dogs. No women. No room for anything but the Fight. What is about to happen is pure reality.

Nigel has tasted Gerald's power and come through the ordeal. Unlike those who'd bet on him, he looks confident. He hurls a long right around a lazy guard. McClellan punches down, misses. Benn knocks his head sideways with a heavy right. His best shot yet. McClellan moves away, confused; it should be over by now.

'This motherfucker still there!'

Mancini takes his eyes off the fight for a second. He checks the banshee crowd behind him in the half-dark. 'Christ, Peter,' he says to DeFreitas, 'I don't know what they paid for those seats but every one of the buggers is standing up!'

Benn's eyes are on fire. He wades forward like a man running out of a burning house. Boxing calmly, an opponent faced with such a sight would slide away, regroup, counter. But McClellan is hypnotised. The energy of the fight sweeps him up. It is Benn — Benn the Survivor — who is setting the agenda that will stay in place for the rest of the fight. So, Gerald's pit-bull instincts and his pride tell him to stand his ground. He has turned into his brother Todd.

They trade headshots. McClellan waltzes away again. Moves left, then right, behind a jab that sings. Benn looks over McClellan's shoulder to Frank Bruno. Big Frank, too big for his suit as always, leads the oral mayhem. Standing up, he unsights half the hall. Flanked by Don King, grin gone, and Frank Warren, deadpan. Naseem Hamed sits impassively.

Benn hooks like a street fighter; McClellan jabs like a matador. Another

street-fighting hook finds Gerald's jaw, a right goes behind him on to his thin,
exposed neck. The American complains. Asaro ignores him. The fighters
clash heads. Benn uppercuts inside. Gerald moves him back to a corner,
uppercuts in reply, into Nigel's forward-leaning torso. They swap missed
rights, clinch, look for a rest. McClellan's slick, long lefts slide over Benn's
bobbing head. Benn shakes him with a left, two rights. The second one spins
him sideways. Another left. Gerald hangs on. Benn goes inside, works the ribs.
Round nearly over. Nigel on top. He hooks to the body, like a vandal chipping
away at some Greek statue. For the first time Gerald's mouthpiece slips from
the grip of his bony jaw. He sucks at the sickly air. Eyes blink. Sweat. Pain.
Doubt.

Benn hits McClellan flush in the teeth, through the exposed mouthguard.
He can't miss. McClellan can't land. Skips left, right. Needs a friend. Looks
for Stan. Benn, pumped, is happier now. This is his manor, no doubt.

I first met Benn, away from the boxing press conferences and the
ring environment, at a beauty contest in an East End nightclub in
the late eighties. Al Hamilton, who'd gone out with Frank Bruno's
sister, was the organiser of Miss London Caribbean. He'd asked me
to be a judge, along with the footballer Robbie Earle and the sports
writer Ronnie Shillingford. There were maybe a thousand people
in the club, on Lower Clapton Road, and I think mine might have
been one of half a dozen white faces. Benn was there, along with
most of the black sporting stars of the capital: John Barnes, Ricky
Hill, Paul Ince – and Ince's cousin, Nigel Benn. Well, Nigel would
claim years later that they were cousins. Ambrose Mendy reckoned
it was a publicity stunt they'd dreamt up for Nigel's return fight
with Chris Eubank at Old Trafford, where Ince was a Manchester
United star. Mendy was still in the Benn camp then. I wasn't going
to get in the middle of that row, though.

Ten years on, and Nigel politely reckons he remembers that first
meeting. Maybe it was my indisputable whiteness that stood out.
Whatever, it's a long time ago and we settle down to reminisce
about his career. It's October 1999, more than four years after the
McClellan fight. Benn's autobiography, *The Dark Destroyer*, is fresh
on the shelves of Waterstone's in Piccadilly and we are parked at a

table in the top-floor restaurant as lunchtime diners grab occasional glances at this vibrant presence. The eyes that burned so fiercely when he fought Gerald and all the others are still on fire. He is a little rounder but not overly so. Benn carries the aura of celebrity without looking self-conscious.

He grew up in Ilford but, sitting opposite me now in a hugely cool and expensive suit, the whole city is his. Not to mention Miami and LA, and Ibiza, where he spins records in nightclubs. Benn moves as comfortably in metropolitania as he once did in the boxing ring. It would appear he has survived the fight game.

While he remembered Clapton ten years earlier, he did not remember that we had spoken more recently. Three days before, in fact, in the basement of Dennie Mancini's Lonsdale shop in nearby Beak Street. Nigel owed Dennie. It was Mancini, after all, who kidded him he was winning the McClellan fight at the end of the first round. Nigel had been in the shop signing copies of his autobiography. A clutch of boxing writers – Colin Hart of the *Sun*, Dave Field of the Press Association, Mike Sinclair of the *Express*, Ian Gibb of the *Mail on Sunday*, and myself – turned up. Ten years earlier, even five, every sports writer in town would have been there. Nigel had broken off briefly from signing and, working his way through the crocodile of fans who stretched up the stairs and out into the shop above, he had come over and hugged us, one by one.

Now, a few days later, we resumed our conversation. He was preoccupied in the way celebrities often are in public. First, he sent back his roast beef sandwich because the waitress could not find mayonnaise for it. She said they had no mayonnaise. He wasn't rude, just firm. She came back a few minutes later with the same sandwich. And the mayonnaise.

He was happy to talk. About the book, of course, about McClellan, about fighting, orgies, his kids, his wife, his enemies. And his dad. 'My dad. I tell you,' says Nigel, 'my old man is hard.' He says 'hard' like he loves the word. 'Haaaard!'

'He was great for me. I needed a man like that, who was going to show me the ropes, the hard way, because, at the end of the day, I'm the fighter and it's good to have my dad around me to steer me in the right direction. When I got nicked for this and that, I would say to the police, "God, phone anybody else but my dad." My dad, he said, "By hook or by crook, you will not end up a criminal."'

Chuck Palahniuk would have liked Nigel's father.

Dickson sounded like Emmite. Two hard fathers determined that their talented, headstrong sons would recognise the disciplines of their chosen sport, would not waste what they had been given. They had not had the chance themselves to be champions but, much as Tiger Woods's father drove his son so relentlessly, they would make sure their kids had every opportunity. Mothers feel this way too, but, in this case, it was more appropriate that the fathers should take the leading role. This was men's work.

'My dad grafted, working his butt off, and he had to look after us as well, you know? Seven hard-core boys. Everyone loved him to death. He is the backbone of the family. He is well respected. I'm like my dad. That's why I speak out, I'm a lot like my dad. If I don't like somebody, I'll speak out. If my dad don't like somebody, he'll tell them he don't like 'em. Simple as that.'

Would his father have been a good fighter?

'Hmm. Strange question. Dunno. He's hard, well hard. But to be a fighter you also need to want to do it. And you need the discipline. I've always been streetwise, but I went in the army too. I know what it's about.'

Benn easily made the distinction between hardness, in the street sense, and boxing grit. It was a judgement that identified how difficult a thing boxing is. It can sap the spirit of the toughest man, especially if he is deficient in the basic skills. I suspect Dickson would have given it a fair shot.

When Dickson Benn and his wife Mina were watching their brood growing up in Ilford, Nigel did not aspire to sainthood. He had more earthly heroes. His brother Andy, for instance. I mistakenly had always thought it was one of his other brothers, John, who inspired him when he spoke of his 'big brother'. John went into the army and Nigel, much to the relief of his parents, followed him. But it was Andy that Nigel loved more than anyone.

When Dickson emigrated to Britain in 1956 from Shorey Village, St Andrew, in Barbados, he was twenty-three and a hard-working, moderately religious man. He left Mina behind so he could set up a new life for them in London. As was often the case in the Caribbean community, she followed a year later once her husband had found work and a place to live. Andy was born not long after Dickson set sail, and, when Mina left, he stayed in Shorey, brought up by his grandmother. They often wish he had not come to London, where his combative nature found too many outlets. Andy was a fight waiting to happen. He first saw his father when he was eight years old. Dickson struggled to keep him in line, much as Emmite struggled with Todd.

Back in Shorey village, in the northern part of tiny, pretty Anglicised Barbados, Dickson had cut cane and worked as a carpenter. In Britain, he became an engineer on the railways. He moved on, becoming an expert tiler; then, like Emmite McClellan, he built car engines, working at the Ford plant in Dagenham. He retired in 1992. It was mildly ironic, given the wild bunch he fathered, that what Dickson really wanted to be was a policeman.

It wasn't easy. The Benns bought a three-bedroomed house in Henley Road in 1960 and, at the time of writing, still live there. For years, whatever the size of Nigel's bank account and his requests for her to retire, Mina kept working. Dickson often had two jobs. Money was tight. Later, he became a born-again Christian. As would Nigel. 'Please, Lord,' Dickson used to pray, 'let me live long enough to see my boys grow up.' Andy didn't quite make it.

He was in and out of borstal and, by seventeen, had a girlfriend twice his age. Like Todd McClellan, Andy ran with a hard crowd. He was not a follower like Todd, though. He was the rarely challenged leader.

Nigel was eight when Andy died. Even now, nobody's sure what happened. Andy was seventeen, the eldest of seven children, all boys. 'He was handsome, powerful and invincible,' Nigel writes. 'Andy could do no wrong. I would feel safe and contented snuggling up to his strong frame, gently bringing my lips to his face and daring to lick or suck his eyebrow while stroking his cheek.'

This is Nigel's account in his book of how Andy died.

We were told that Andy had been visiting his girlfriend and

that there had been a disturbance at her house. There is a suggestion that a number of people had grouped together in another room and that Andy considered a quick escape to be preferable to an unfairly matched battle. He is said to have leapt from an upstairs window, hoping to clear a glass conservatory room and land in the garden from where he could jump over the back fence. In his rush, he fell through the conservatory roof, shattering the glass and severing a main artery in his groin. Did anyone try to help him as he bled to death? That is another question that continues to trouble me but may never be answered. We all wept for him then and I still grieve for him now. There have been times when I have thought very seriously of joining him prematurely, to hold him close to me once more. If death means that there is a chance of being with my brother again, then I am tempted towards that unknown journey.

This melancholia has been common in Nigel's life. When his first marriage was breaking up and he was living in America, he says he considered suicide. He sought professional help and is candid about the troubled side of his personality. He doesn't sound flippant when he says he has no fear of death. Maybe that was his armour in the boxing ring. He understood the language Gerald was talking, no doubt. In war you die.

Nigel and his other brothers were not allowed to go to Andy's funeral, because Dickson and Mina wanted them to remember him alive and healthy, a strong force in a tight-knit family. The brothers still do not know where in Barkingside Cemetery Andy is buried.

So, eight years old, Nigel took to the streets. He fought hard and often. As he points out, though, he was not even supposed to be a boy. Dickson and Mina had wanted a girl to stop an unbroken run of five boys. They were sure their prayers were going to be answered when a gypsy came calling when Mina was pregnant and predicted her next baby should be fitted up for frilly pink knickers. So seriously did Dickson take the reality of a sixth son that he wrecked a red telephone booth near the house. A passing neighbour witnessed the one-man riot and calmly remarked to Dickson, 'It's another boy, then, Mr Benn?'

It was the winter of 1964, a Wednesday morning, 22 January, when Nigel Gregory Benn started his journey. Besides Andy, he joined Dermot, five years older, John, three years older, Danny, two years older, and Mark, just a year older. Six years later, Anthony rounded out the clan.

Woodlands Infant School was the first to tackle the Benn frenzy. Then Cleveland Primary, where he refined his bullying among older boys. At Loxford School, his reputation grew.

Nigel had his first proper fight when he was nine. He remembers the time and the place and the opponent: at the local swimming pool against Leo Isaacs, who was twelve. Nigel got his career off to a winning start with a right-hander 'straight in the eye' . . .

Nigel nudges his quarter-eaten sandwich around the plate, swishes back his beaded hair and stretches out in his chair. He is a man totally at ease with his occupation of space. People move aside for Nigel Benn. It is not intimidation, more territorial squatting. He was always slight for a super-middleweight, having trained into the shape that took him to twelve stone, mixing Spartan preparation with bursts of crazy clubbing. He doesn't mind a drink. And he definitely does like his food. There is not much spare on him, though. His natural fitness keeps him within a stone of his fighting weight. His face is scarred up – from the streets more than the ring – and his knuckles carry the calluses of his calling like diamond nuggets.

Retirement suits him. He had some tax problems years ago, and moved to Barbados for sanctuary. But his house in Peckham is grand, introduced to passers-by by two large panther statues at the driveway gate. Inside is his mixing studio, where he works on his DJing. The Ministry of Sound might be his powerbase now, but Benn is forever a fighting man. He is not someone to 'mess with'. When he fell out with his great friend, Rolex Ray, assault charges ensued. Benn got off. But, pick a fight, verbal or physical, and you are in for a hard time.

Time to get to the heart of the matter. Had he ever watched the McClellan fight since that night?

'Once. Just showed it to my friends. Can't really watch it . . .'

This is one of those moments in an interview when you detect more through silence than words. We look at each other, he almost daring me to press it. I decline. I know he is emotional; all the testimony of his private life points to it. I believe, also, that he cares about McClellan. It would be a cruel man who didn't. But we handle our past in different ways. Psychologists might call Benn's reluctance to dwell on the fight 'denial'. They could be right. I'm no psychologist. I'm just looking at a retired fighter mulling over whether or not to articulate his feelings about the worst night of his career. I let the silence talk . . . and then he fills the gap, matter-of-factly:

'But I do want to get a collection of all my fights. To me it was just work. The best fight of my life, everybody had me to lose, from the *Telegraph* down to the *Sun*, the *Mirror*, the *Star*. To go in, dig down and come up with that – man! Still I had nothing to prove, only to myself, to prove how strong I was, and how determined. I'm not one of these Brits that's going to lie down. I'll have it on with anyone. You'll get a lot of boxers out there who can beat me, but you won't get a lot who can fight me. You can get people out there who can box my head off but you won't get a lot of people who can stand there and have it with me.'

It's not unusual for retired fighters to continue to talk about themselves as if they were still active. Benn will always be a fighter, whether he is licensed or not. As will McClellan. But he sidesteps the aftermath. What is significant for him, as far as handling the experience, is the actual fighting. It was the mountain peak of everything that mattered to him. It was the performance of a lifetime and he is not keen to talk about it in any other context than that which is pertinent to his craft of boxing. To do so lessens what he achieved. He cannot put Gerald's injuries alongside it. He has to compartmentalise the two happenings. Who am I to say that he is right or wrong?

I wanted to know what he had thought of McClellan before the fight? Again he responds in purely boxing terms:

'Nothin'. Never even thought nothin' about him. I always thought . . . I was just thinking about myself. I was never worried about him, never worried about him whatsoever. I was more interested in myself, that all the training was right, everything was spot on. I just knew, I just knew . . . He, remember, had moved up from light-middleweight, to middleweight to super-middleweight. He'd done it real fast, but it had taken me a whole year to move from middleweight to super-middleweight. I was very scared about moving up to that weight. I wasn't even a big middleweight. I was always small but I knew for a fact that I had the power and I had the guts to match them all, the will to win. A lot of them didn't have that.'

This will sound callous to some, especially so to Gerald's family. But fighters often talk coldly about what they do. If they didn't, they would go crazy. A lot of people reckon they're half-crazy anyhow. And they are. They are a certain sort of crazy. They experience highs and lows that few of us will approach. They are special by the nature of their business. When they win, when they experience the joy of physical dominance, the power of a knockout, they are more alive than anyone they have ever known – except other boxers; when they lose, when they are knocked out or marginalised by boxing's powerbrokers, they embrace desolation that, thankfully, only a few of us will experience. Nigel – and Gerald – have been to both places.

Even in retirement, there is a belligerence about Benn. Someone who has had her share of confrontations with him is his second wife, Carolyne. As we talk, he declares his love for her. A few days later, another woman comes from nowhere to tell a tabloid paper about their nights of passion in Ibiza, where Nigel was DJing. Never a dull moment with Nigel. Later, he would confess he had again con-sidered suicide, so guilty did he feel about his womanising.

'I got all this from my wife,' he says of his settled state. 'If it wasn't for her, I'd be skint. I'd be fighting now. She come along, there's forty grand here, three hundred grand there, tax bills, all sorts of things, she sorted it. She's my wife. Anything I own, she owns. It's all hers as well. Without her I'd end up like all the boxers, punchy and with no money in the bank. It's sad. That's why a lot of managers, promoters get away with things.'

There's a bit of sandwich left. Nigel scoffs it in one go. He does not miss the regime that made him such a good fighting machine. And he can talk about that all night.

'When I used to train, I lived on boiled chicken, all that sort of stuff, 150 to 180 vitamins a day, and sometimes I had to eat fish for breakfast. I had this nutritionist from Blackpool, he told me what I had to do. But it was horrible. Sometimes I'd get it down there and they'd just about have their foot down my throat feeding me and I'd say, "No man, it's horrible," and I'd sick it all up! But then I kept on trying, kept on trying, to get it down until I did it. Then after that, after six weeks of it, of vigorous training, I could eat what I want, kebabs, fish and chips, whatever. I let myself go right down. No place in the middle. That's how I done my training.

'But I done it because I wanted my mum and dad to be proud of me. All their life they've been grafters. I'd say, "Why don't you go away, have a dirty weekend in France with Dad or something?" And she'd say, "No, I gotta look after my grandkids." You know?'

The women in Nigel's life – and there have been a few – have never had a quiet time of it.

'Carolyne wanted me to retire three years before I did. When we met, she didn't even know who I was. When she did find out, she never took a penny from me. I went to put £500 in her pocket and she wouldn't have it. There was a cheque for $400,000 and she gave it straight back. She's been through a lot with me and I'll owe her for the rest of my life.

'I'm very hard and I'm very soft at the same time. Sharron [Benn's first wife] used to make me cry. I know it's not very English – stiff upper lip and that. With Carolyne and the baby though, I'm learning every day. I'm trying to learn about it all. Fighters are very emotional. A lot of people don't see that. They might look at me, say, and say, well, he's an animal – but there's another side to me. Fighting is a very emotional experience.'

There have always been celebrities crowding about the ring apron of boxing. Celebs (mostly of the B-list variety), writers, promoters, boxers, bouncers, hangers-on and mums and dads. A lot of people at ringside thought that first-hand count on Nigel a bit tight. One of them was not Dickson Benn.

McClellan would apparently sort him out too once he got through with Nigel.

As Lisa says, it's all talk. But talk still hurts.

Mr Benn sat/stood right behind me, but he was not a man to ask if his son had just cheated the clock in the first round of the biggest fight of his life. His eyes were popping like the buttons on Bruno's suit. He risked shredding his vocal cords. I just hoped he didn't start thumping my back. As it was, the copytaker typing out the running copy at the other end was struggling to hear my desperate commentary.

Next to Dickson, less agitated, sat Patsy Palmer. An *EastEnders* soap star. Grew up not far away from here. A real East Ender. Her thin, freckled face, red hair and unbelieving eyes belonged to an ingénue. Patsy's screams were soprano lead to Dickson's basso profundo. What a caterwaul. She was happy to be here. This was an event.

The inner ring was full of models and champs and ex-champs. But ex-champs have clout in various dwindling amounts. Like an old pug trying for one more title shot. If you're a very ex-champ, you struggle for a comp. Have to almost beg, sometimes. If you're a recent ex-champ and you're hot, or reasonably warm, with a current TV ad maybe, or you're on the after-dinner circuit, no problem. Take two tickets. Bring a friend. As long as they're famous.

Henry Cooper, although very ex, is top of the old fighters' pile – they pay him £5,000 a night to speak at some dos; except he'd soon stop coming to the fights. Didn't like Naz and his entrances, for a start. Cooper got fed up at Wembley a couple of months after this one, the night Bruno finally won the world heavyweight title, the night he beat Oliver McCall quicker than the crack cocaine could. DeFreitas claims to have seen McCall 'on it' at a famous West End club after that fight. Frank took so long to get to the ring, Henry wasn't having it any longer.

I'd seen him calm the mob the night Tony Sibson lost to the pretty good American Frank Tate. With a simple, honest speech from centre ring, Henry stopped a riot by a crew of geniuses who'd come up from London with CS gas canisters. For someone who used to go out walking near his south London home during the

Blitz, who'd been carved to pieces by Muhammad Ali, who'd given his life to the hardest spot, it wasn't a big deal taming a herd of boneheads.

But Henry was bored with it. Bored with the showbiz. Bored with the glamour. Still, he was not going to miss the night Nigel fought Gerald.

Footballers are always in there. They could afford to buy row upon row of £1,000 seats, but they like to be asked along for free. It's the power-celeb Mexican stand-off. Hard to explain a Mexican: if you're famous and you ring the promoter for a free one, you might get edged out – too keen. That's a straight-up Mexican. If you're famous and you don't ring, and you still miss out, that can be a Double Mexican; the promoter's called your bluff. But, if you want a ticket, don't ring up and he still gives you a ticket, that might be a rare Reverse Triple Mexican. The easiest way to get into the fights, of course, is to actually be a Mexican. When it comes down to it, if you're a face, make the best of it.

There was a model sitting next to Patsy who looked familiar. But not with her clothes on. The testosterone levels at boxing are considerable and she was not doing much to restore the sexual equilibrium. Out further back were the rest of them. Hot, mad and screaming. Where the unscheduled fight had broken out earlier, they were bunched up. Sweating conspirators in the dark. A giant, umbilically linked knot of heartbeats. They stared down at Nigel and they will have noticed how skinny the champ's legs looked. Benn never was a fancy mover, his inward-turning feet almost tripping over themselves as he shuffled forward to hook, cross, jab, sway low. Just like Tyson. But he was diligent. He worked on his balance and lateral movement, especially when he was hanging out in the gyms in Miami.

First round, Nigel had looked anything but clever as Newbon's microphone almost disappeared up his backside. That would be a hell of a way to lose your world title. If you saw Nigel in that state in the street – glassy-eyed, off his head and staggering on plasticine legs – you'd walk around him. Give the wino some distance. And, in a way, he was just that – intoxicated, beyond redemption, high on fighting.

Going to war: 'Walking from the locker room to the ring is the scariest feeling I ever had in my life.' © Vanessa Winship.

There was something going on behind the scarred visage, though, and it had nothing to do with congratulating Gerald on a good right cross. Nigel, wounded and ready to uncoil, was on for the tear-up of tear-ups. That's why round two was so scary. Whenever he'd been hurt in the past, Benn had exacted terrible retribution on the other fighter.

The first of these, the one Benn fans remember best, was Anthony Logan, who'd knocked Nigel's brains into mini-mash at the Royal Albert Hall in round two of their fight in October 1988. Benn had spent only thirty-five rounds winning his first eighteen fights and had not been inconvenienced, but, once Logan landed, he could have been sunning himself back in Shorey village, for all he knew. He fell in a screaming heap, an ugly incomprehension filling his face. Somehow he righted himself and started to rise, a holed destroyer listing violently. At about the sixty-degree mark, his right glove still touching the canvas, he looked out past the ring lights, through the ropes and, above the tumult, he could hear only his mother yelling from the safety of the shore: 'Stop the fight! Stop the fight!' In Ilford, this was uncool.

'She stopped going to my fights after that,' Benn said later. 'I said, "Mum, don't ever come to one of my fights again!" Can you imagine it: Nigel Benn's mum, come to bail him out. No way! No way! She won't even watch it on TV. She'll go out in the street, walk around the corner for about half an hour or so. You don't want your mum getting all upset, especially when she's got high blood pressure.'

Her husband looked as embarrassed as their son.

Then Nigel got angry. The Dark Destroyer dragged his fight-settler up from the floor and flung it at Logan's impassive face. On impact, the Jamaican's features were instantly distorted and he went over like an overcoat slung in the corner. Counted out.

Benn's legend grew twenty feet. Every one of his fights after that one would be judged by that punch. And, except for the night when he took a ten-count on the end of Michael Watson's stiff jab at Finsbury Park in 1989, Nigel always got up. Mancini was in Watson's corner that night. 'Nigel didn't so much swallow it – it was only a left jab that put him down – as wear himself out. I think there was a lot going on at that time. He wasn't right for the fight. It looked like exhaustion at the end.'

The Watson loss only made him stronger, however. He couldn't bear to hear people say he'd dogged it. The pain was so bad he almost quit boxing. A jab – how could a jab keep Nigel Benn on the floor? The question swirled about boxing for weeks, and a lot of fans were ready to consign Benn to the bin. He'd been good, he'd been worth the ticket, but he'd bottled it. That was the word. Where Nigel grew up, you didn't bottle it and show your face the next day. There were things they didn't know about that fight, though. Like a bad haircut. We'll come to that.

Now, at Docklands, he'd got up again. He'd got back into the fight. This was McClellan, not Watson. Those of us who'd seen a lot of his fights knew we were in for what Jim Rosenthal had identified as 'something special'. I wasn't sure Gerald knew what he was in for. But Harry knew. 'We've got some fight on our hands now.'

Harry Mullan, silvery rascal of our fight-writing fraternity, loved and loathed Nigel and his like, for the power this sort of fighter held over him, for the animalism of his boxing. And there was something hypnotic about the pigeon-toed thrasher from Ilford that made it impossible to look away. Tonight at Docklands was Nigel's night of nights, the night you would not look away from for all the money you could spend. This was why we were here.

Reg Gutteridge: 'This is the old Dark Destroyer now.'

Jim Watt: 'It looks better for Benn. He's starting to get some power into the punches. A good shot from Benn! A good left hook, that's exactly what he needs.'

Gutteridge: 'McClellan's complaining about a rabbit blow there on the back of the neck.'

It would not be the last. Benn doesn't worry about the niceties. He ploughs on, slinging, dipping, thumping.

Watt: 'He's getting punches through now and shaking McClellan up. McClellan is looking a little bit sloppy in this round, Reg, as though he felt the fight was over . . . Another terrific left hook from Benn!'

Gutteridge: 'There's some sweaty palms around here, fidgeting at ringside. Now which one is going to go first? Benn looked like he had more chance of surviving a firing squad in the first round, but he's got over it. He's had a good second round.'

4

From the Boardwalk to the Strip in Under Five Minutes

'Ain't nothing worse than a dog in baahxin'. A dog let you down.
Everybody hate a dog. That's the way Gerald saw it too . . .' – Some-
body in a bar in Chicago, gone midnight.

The G-Man did not go out of his way for the TV cameras and,
looking back over his early years as a paid fighter, he came across
as almost dull when he wasn't crushing brain cells. Never said ten
words where none would do. Gerald was just short of rude and he
didn't much worry about that. As long as he got his cheque.

This attitude would perplex the television promoters. They
want a knockout artist, but they would like a bit of 'personality' to
go with their product. Still, what they suspected was that there was
steel in his sullen mien. The G-Man would not let them down in
the ring. Gerald was what his sister Lisa called 'a piece of work'.

The start to McClellan's career should have been that of a
groomed and favoured prospect. After all, despite missing the
Olympics in 1988, he was an exceptional amateur and by now he
was hooked up with Manny Steward at the Kronk, the most famous
gym in the world. His career didn't so much fly at first, however, as
glide into a swamp.

He had a couple of tune-ups, in Milwaukee and Glen Burnie. A
round apiece against fighters their mothers wouldn't remember.
Then came the call to boxing's capital – Las Vegas. This, thought
Gerald, was what it was about. Someone called Danny Lowry went
over in a round. Three weeks later, Gerald was entertaining the
high-rollers again, putting Ezequiel Obando away in the first. He
liked Vegas. He could smell wealth, and glamour. Lot of good-
looking women in Vegas, too. Yet he wasn't at ease.

The deal with Manny is this: he's the boss. Lennox Lewis and
Naseem Hamed would learn that. As Evander Holyfield had.

The G-Man, aware of his image but not overly concerned with the media, talks the talk for the showdown with Benn. © Vanessa Winship.

There are not two ways of doing things, just Manny's. Gerald wanted to go with Sugar Ray Leonard in the first instance, but when he saw Leonard leaning towards Roy Jones Jr and when Jones went to Seoul instead of him, Gerald got mad. He knew then he wouldn't be taking Stan with him on his journey into the pros, because he needed a fresh start after his amateur career had stalled near the hilltop. And that's how Gerald made it to Detroit, and Stan stayed on the other side of those tracks.

After Steward had given him a taste of Vegas, however, he took McClellan off to Auburn Hills, near Detroit, for another cakewalk. And Cleveland. Ditto. And Biloxi (KO 2), Waukesha (KO 1), Monessen (TKO 2), Milwaukee (TKO 1). He was getting $300 for some of these fights. He was losing motivation. The kid who had to be bullied to spar with his brother under the street lights in Freeport was starting to kick at the system. As, at that time, was Nigel Benn, who was working his way through what he called his 'Mexican roadsweepers' (none of whom was Mexican, for the record). Nigel was feeding on the likes of Darren Hobson and Mbayo Wa Mbayo; Gerald had Joe Goodman. Jerome Kelly. John Gordon.

Ten fights. Ten wins. Easy. Too easy. And then . . . defeat. On 24 June 1989, in Atlantic City, Dennis Milton beat McClellan on points over six rounds. The G-Man could not believe it.

How could this be? Maybe there was a flaw. Losing to an outsider was not a crime, but it didn't look good, for his credibility or his confidence. Until that blip, McClellan had had it his own way, in common with all big hitters with a pedigree. In his first ten contests, he'd scored four clean knockouts, three of them in the first round. He had six wins that forced the referee to save his pummelled opponents, four in the first round and two in the second. So, between his debut in Milwaukee on 12 August 1988, when he iced Roy Huntley in the first, until he stopped Terrence Wright in round one eight months later in Atlantic City, Gerald had barely had a workout. Gerald had always told Todd smarts would beat power. Now he was finding out what a good analyst of boxing he was.

They used to call Milton 'the Magician'. Born in the Bronx, he'd boxed in good company up and down the eastern seaboard, turning pro in '85 after being rated the best amateur light-middleweight in the country. By the time he was served up for McClellan, he still had a respectable sheet, eleven wins against two losses and a draw, but he shouldn't have presented a problem. That summer of '89, though, Milton was too sparky for Gerald over six rounds.

In the boxing scheme of things, Gerald was entitled to repair his career against undemanding opposition. Unfortunately, he picked the wrong guy. Ralph Ward of Ohio was a fighter whose name was more redolent of an American fifties sitcom than the fight game. He was twenty-six, with no ring nickname, but he could fight a bit and was still ambitious. He came to the fight that September with a record not unlike Milton's: eleven wins and three losses – crucially, in the fight before the McClellan fixture, Ralph had been beaten over ten rounds by Terry Norris, a considerable ring presence.

Again, a lacklustre McClellan got slicked out of it, decisioned over eight rounds. Like the Magician, Ralph would go on a losing spree after getting himself up for Gerald. His chin had stood up well in the first phase of his career, but now it let him down. He started losing, put the gloves away for six years and the last that was heard of him was in a down-the-bill comeback at Lake Charles in 1998, when one Willie Williams stopped him in the second.

Before Christmas of '89, Gerald went home to Freeport to think about his future. He told his local paper, 'I had a bad attitude. I wasn't doing anything and I couldn't get along with anybody. So I said, "Let me give it one more try – three strikes and you're out." '

Another trailer-load of opponents came and went in 1990. They lined them up and he knocked them down. Gerald injured his knee in February 1991, but he kept going. He didn't want that third strike. TV still wanted a piece of him and he knew he'd get his chance sooner or later. Meanwhile, the G-Man was starting to ask hard questions of Steward, Davimos and King. He was running out of patience.

In November, McClellan came to London for the first time and put a shadow of the once-awesome John Mugabi away in a round to win the World Boxing Organisation's version of the mid-dleweight championship. He impressed his London audience with the ruthlessness of his finishing, even if the title was more cardboard than gold and the opponent was shot.

Mugabi had been a terrific light-middleweight, a world champion. Even when he moved up to middleweight, he gave Marvin Hagler a tough time – but he came into this fight all torn up, upstairs and down. He had been in a bad car accident not long before and the rising Terry Norris had knocked him out in the first round of his previous fight at light-middleweight. Mugabi would end up fighting in Australia years later for derisory sums.

McClellan looked his usual awesome self in knocking Mugabi down three times and the title was OK, but not enough. He hungered for the genuine big time. The WBO meant nothing to him. Where were the big fights, he wanted to know, the big money? Why wasn't he fighting Jones? On 15 May 1992, he got another low-key TV gig . . . back on the boardwalk. He was being yo-yoed. If he didn't start making a noise, he'd get shuffled. Like Stan had been.

Atlantic City is a rich dump like no other. Along the seafront, it could be Blackpool. The sea crashes, the fruit machines flash and pop, offering more than they deliver. Blue-collar workers stroll up and down, taking in the tack. Go a couple of hundred yards into the hinterland, however, behind the casinos and . . . well, don't. It's the gambling and the fights they come for. It's not Vegas but it's the East Coast's own.

'Ladies and gentlemen, live from the Mark Etess Arena at the Trump Taj Mahal in Atlantic City . . .' It was a downbeat evening all round, despite the best efforts of the TV warm-up man.

Gerald, a headliner in London, a world champion of sorts, was back on the undercard. Topping the bill was Michael Moorer, whom he'd beaten in the amateurs and with whom he shared a trainer and a manager. Moorer was a strange one. He wanted to be a cop, but his association with the law was often on the wrong side of the counter. He created trouble. He wore a T-shirt with the message, *You have the right to remain violent.* Michael, a quality fighter from the Kronk, was one of Manny's problem kids. Tonight he was fighting Smokin' Bert Cooper for the vacant WBO heavyweight title. When a world heavyweight title is vacant, it's nearly always because nobody wants it.

Gerald had given up his own WBO title and was marking time in a non-title ten-rounder, unusual in itself. His opponent was Carl 'the Irish Assassin' Sullivan. This was where Gerald's career had become becalmed. A win over Sullivan would do little for his cause, even if it topped up his credit cards. The Assassin had won twelve, lost four, with eight KOs, the defining statistic for the networks. He'd lost three of his previous four fights – all by stoppage. 'Not a hot boxer,' confided Larry Berman at the mike.

Roy Jones, meanwhile, was pulling away from Gerald. He'd come home from Seoul a martyr, the victim of outrageous judging, and signed a big contract to turn professional. Where Gerald was quiet, sometimes sullen, Jones had a mouthy edge – but TV liked him, and even used him in ads to promote their boxing programmes. He was being groomed while Gerald was being ignored. Jones had stopped one-time world champion Jorge Vaca in a round in January, knocked out the useful Art Serwano in the first . . . and, within a year, he'd be getting the better of Bernard 'the Executioner' Hopkins over twelve to win the International Boxing Federation middleweight belt.

'We expect a near full house here tonight,' said TVKO's Khambrel Marshall, standing in a hall that was not remotely crowded. WNBC New York were doing the commentary duties ringside. 'The moral tonight, if you're a boxer,' said Berman, 'is always be prepared. Three of our six boxers tonight only got the call to arms in the past seven days.' We were definitely parked on big-time boxing's hard shoulder.

Sullivan hadn't fought in nearly a year and calcium was building up like a bad debt on his experienced knuckles. Gerald's was hardly a royal progress and not many people seemed concerned.

His fight with Carl was first up. It wouldn't take long. Gerald moved up to the red corner wearing the US Marine red-and-gold of the Kronk, and Steward was his smiling, guiding light. If the fighter was treading water, he at least was in good hands. To lend menace to his appearance, the G-Man was announced as fighting 'out of the Motor City!'. Statistically he was fine: 164 pounds, 24–2 with twenty-two KOs, all inside three rounds. 'Don't blink when it comes to Gerald McClellan,' viewers were told.

The twenty-four-year-old Gerald was announced at 6ft 1in, but actually was 6ft, his reach was given as seventy-nine inches, but was really seventy-seven. Anyway, he was a couple of inches taller and a year younger than the outgunned Assassin, who was resplendent in emerald green – Gerald's favourite colour, as it happened.

I'd asked Lisa about the family antecedents. Any Irish, with the Mc? 'Probably. Couldn't say.' Unlike Tyson. Or Ali. Irish or not, Gerald jabbed with speed and power this night. Bolts. Liston-like. Sullivan threw one jab, into McClellan's gloves. Another range-finding right winged the air. McClellan followed his left with a right to the side of Carl's chops, and Sullivan's legs bid his brain adios. A few more swipes through and over the Pittsburghian's guard, with a finishing left hook – as Al Moreland had taught him – and the Irish Assassin was going nowhere but home to Momma's stew. It took forty-five seconds, a TVKO record, Gerald's twenty-third knockout.

The officials were all provided locally – Frank Brunette, from Rahway, Richard Strange from Bricktown and Atlantic City's own Eugenia 'Jean' Williams, later to achieve notoriety at the Garden as one of the most inept boxing officials of modern times, when she picked Evander Holyfield over Lennox Lewis against the almost universal view to the contrary. None of them was ever going to be needed. Tony Perez, the referee, helped pick up Sullivan, but otherwise this was all Gerald's own handiwork. As with a lot of Gerald's early fights, he could have settled it over the phone. The right he hit Sullivan with was cleaner but longer than the one that would put Nigel through the ropes.

Gerald had thrown fifteen punches, eleven landing; Carl threw two, both appeared to miss, the second ever televised shutout on TVKO – although the winner was gracious enough later to credit Sullivan with maybe brushing his left eye. 'Nothin',' Gerald says. 'He mighta caught me with a right hand across the top of my eye, a hook or something. It stings a little. But it wasn't much.'

Stings a little. Odd. I've looked at the tape several times, and the only blow Sullivan came even close to landing was a reluctant dab with his right that might have brushed Gerald's left eye. But it was a gnat nipping a tiger, if that. Yet Gerald reckoned it 'stings a little'.

Superficially at least, something might not have been right. His expression looked drained, his eyes those of a man whose concerns were elsewhere. He may have known, even then, that inside his head, the parts weren't working properly. It's impossible to ask him now.

In his post-fight interview he was happy, but hardly jumping out of his skin. 'I was always going to take my time, to box, work the jab up and down, and I'd find an opening somewhere, and the openin' came and I went for it. I work on my jab a lot, on the heavy bag, tryin' to master it, up and down, hook off the jab, and it worked for me.'

Regulation fightspeak.

'I was just tellin' Manny, I have a tendency every time I land the right hand on the chin, I just turn and walk before the opponent falls, because I'm so confident. But tonight I came back and jumped on him.'

Since winning his world title the previous November, Gerald had jumped on Lester Yarbrough in a round, at Auburn Hills in February; after Sullivan, he'd jump on poor Steve Harvey at Lake Tahoe in a round the next November; then he'd go to Mexico City in the February of '93 to jump on the unfortunate Tyrone Moore (TKO 2). More no-names.

These were dustbin fights. If a good fighter has too many of them, he loses his sharpness. He becomes complacent. If he is being fed what the industry unkindly calls tomato cans, he might cheat on his training. If unstretched in the ring, he will be unsure of how to handle pressure when it comes. If he has knockout power, he might consider it a waste of time training for any fight longer than a few rounds. It happened to Tyson. And, in a different way, it would happen to Hamed. Back in '91 and '92, the danger was it was happening to McClellan.

Gerald was almost certainly having harder fights in the gym. Already a world champion once, he was learning little. His 'attitude' was getting mean. He'd go missing a lot, demanding that King and Steward and Davimos (who also handled Moorer) get him some serious money or he'd walk, do it all himself. Gerald had no time for the grind of boxing politics. It was the way he was, all day, all night. Never sitting still. Demanding a result at every turn.

'With Gerald,' says Lisa, 'before he got hurt, you could never get him to sit down long enough to find out what was goin' on. You know? He was always in and out, in and out. He'd come to town, and you might see him for five minutes and he'd come over and visit and five minutes later he'd be out the door again. Then you might get a knock on the door at three o'clock in the mornin' and he's comin' back again.'

Gerald always had his other life to lead. He didn't do drugs, didn't give alcohol serious consideration, but he loved his night manoeuvres, his pit-bull dog fights, his trips to the projects with Donnie and Stan and Vicious and Midnight and Manny's minder, Willie Brown.

But finally the waiting would be over. On 8 May 1993, after all those nothing fights, after too long in the sandpit with his toys, it was time to go to work. And Julian Jackson under the big lights in Las Vegas was what any fighter would call work. This was the sort of fight Gerald wanted. And the venue. He had not been back to Vegas to fight since 22 November 1988, an absence from the genuine big time of twenty-five fights and nearly five years. He was back from the boardwalk. While it had taken just a few minutes' work in the ring along the way to get there, there was a lot of spare time packed in around his ring time.

Few contenders relished the prospect of putting it on the line against Jackson, a quiet, religious man from St Thomas in the Virgin Islands. Julian had made his Vegas debut as long ago as May 1983, fully a decade beforehand. He'd been boxing for thirteen years by the time he signed to defend his World Boxing Council middleweight title against McClellan, and he'd chilled forty-three of his opponents along the way. Gerald knew things were getting real.

Showtime were with him too, describing him as the 'heir apparent'. You guessed they'd like the younger man to win, but they wanted the old guy to give a good account of himself too, maybe set up a rematch. Jackson had imposing credentials – the World Boxing Association junior middleweight title from 1987 to 1989 – but a serious optical weakness ought to have disqualified him from fighting. In 1989, he'd undergone surgery to repair detached retinas on both eyes. When he recovered, he gave up the eleven-stone title and moved up to middleweight, even though he was still essentially a light-middle. Jackson was a man with desperation in his milky eyes.

Gerald won the first round, then the champion 'kinda got his momentum goin' in that second round,' McClellan recalled. 'By the end of the round, he had a big finish. So I had to go back to my corner, regroup and start my game plan all over again.'

Jackson remembers it this way: 'When I went back to my corner, I was so confident. I was sayin', "It's just a matter of a couple of rounds now, and I know you'll be finished."'

Jackson kept on top in round three, until a clash of heads left him with a cut on his eye. Now he was angry. 'I wanted to get back at him . . . and I lost control.' The fourth round was uneventful. Then came the fifth, one of the best rounds of boxing in 1993. Jackson hit McClellan low, Gerald took a knee but declined the offer of a long rest by the referee Mills Lane. 'I coulda taken five minutes to recover,' Gerald told Showtime, 'and Julian was lookin' at me, get-tin' stronger and stronger, so I figured the sooner I get up the bet-ter. When I got up, he came right at me, stood right in front of me. That's when I caught him with the right hand and two left hooks.'

Beautiful boxing skills, perfectly applied under pressure in a big championship bout at a venue where it mattered. This exchange should have informed the unknowing that McClellan was an elite fighter, a genuine world-class champion, in any era.

Gerald hit Julian with a sickening right, he went down, it was over.

As Jackson remembers, 'I saw it coming and I couldn't get out of the way, because I was just rushin' in.'

It had been a dream encounter for the bloodthirsty, the match-up of two wicked punchers, the most dangerous, and the most exciting outside the heavyweight division – more so even than Benn, whose power had been blunted since he'd moved up from middleweight. This was the pivotal fight in the boxing entertain-ment business that year. Gerald had a stoppage rate of 91.8 per cent, unmatched in the upper echelons of marketable boxing. He could not be denied from here on. And he liked the way it felt to be the gruesome hitter his middleweight peers wanted to avoid.

'You hit somebody, and you knock 'em out, you knock 'em unconscious, you can tell before the person falls, on his way down . . . a good shot, from a right hand or a left hook, it's a good feelin'. To me, knockin' somebody out, it's like havin' sex . . . you know what I mean? It's a good feelin'.'

It felt good to have a belt again, a proper belt. Now he wanted the money. But, as with nearly any deal involving King, there would be drama. That August, three months after beating the other most-avoided middleweight in the world, Gerald found himself defending his title against an anonymous challenger in a seriously low-key event in Bayamon, Puerto Rico. Jay Bell was not a fighter to frighten a champion – there would be other conflicts on the trip, though.

'When Gerald knocked out that guy Bell in Puerto Rico,' Stan Johnson recalls, 'well, he met this girl Maria Rousseau, who was working with Don King in Florida. She fell in love with Gerald, Gerald fell in love with her. I thought they was good for each other but, like, Gerald had a girlfriend at home he was gonna marry . . .'

According to Stan, the King family objected to Gerald's liaison with Maria. Gerald and Don's stepson Carl had a heated argument, and Carl told him, 'Julian Jackson gonna take care of you soon.' Gerald replied, 'I'll kick Julian Jackson's ass and your ass the next day.'

Stan goes on: 'The King clan didn't like Gerald; they thought he was gettin' cocky, gettin' up in that ring and wantin' to keep all that money to himself. Now I'm the kinda guy, I told Gerald, if a guy's makin' six million and he's givin' me three million and he's stealin' three million, I don't give a fuck. I tell him, "Next time get twelve so you can steal six and get me six." But Gerald wasn't that kinda guy; he didn't want no motherfucker steal from him. You know, he wanted to make all the money. He wanted to be like Sugar Ray Leonard and Muhammad Ali was. Later on in boxing, Ray Leonard controlled his own career. "I'm gonna do this, and I'm gonna get this much and fuck all the rest of you motherfuckers." Huh? Right. Ali did the same thing, but I say, "Gerald, you can't have it like that, you need pay some kinda dues." '

47

Gerald couldn't wait. He was chasing Jones. That would make his career. To get to Jones, he'd have to go through Benn first. But he didn't think that would be a problem. For Gerald, nothing was a problem.

Stan: 'Gerald was sayin', "All I gotta do is knock out Nigel Benn, don't sign this promotional contract with Don King, then this'll be all my money." That's the way he was workin' it out, but boxin' people ain't gonna let you do that. All you got is the talent, you can't play the games, you can't deal with these fuckin' sneaks and sharks out there. They been doin' this shit for years. "They not gonna let you do that, man. They gonna let you go out mad and blind, Gerald, before they let that happen." That's what I said . . . You know what I mean?'

But for now, at least, King and his client wanted the same thing – a better fight for more money. Benn and a move up to twelve stone could weight. So they went and got McClellan the number one middleweight contender, Lamar 'Kidfire' Parks, for what Don reckoned would be 'an absolute barnburner' in Las Vegas in March of 1994. But Kidfire, who'd been promised a million-dollar pay day if he could beat McClellan, never showed up.

On the night, the Showtime commentators told their audience Lamar had pulled out with an injured shoulder. There was a late replacement. It wasn't the whole story. The whole story was awful.

'He was the strongest I'd ever seen,' Lamar's coach Silas Epps told journalist Bruce Schoenfeld a couple of years later. Parks learnt to box in Epps's gym at the Phillis Wheatley Community Center in Greenville, South Carolina. At twenty-three, he was to get his big break. A world-title fight with McClellan. Parks wouldn't talk about what happened, but others did.

In June of '93, Parks had gone to New York to get ready for a fight when he got a call from his girlfriend Samantha Clark. She'd tested positive for HIV. Lamar told her to tell nobody. They'd been seeing each other for a couple of years, although for Lamar it was apparently not an exclusive arrangement. 'I know she's a good woman, Silas,' he told his trainer, 'because she was a virgin when I met her.'

Samantha was not a drug user, so Lamar knew what that meant:

he might have been responsible for what she now had. And for what he had. On 10 August 1993, two months after he got the call from Samantha, Lamar beat Gilbert Baptist in Greenville. Two months later, he knocked out Joaquin Velasquez. He'd won twenty-nine and lost just one, stopping twenty-one opponents. Those credentials earned him his WBC rating and a contract worth $150,000 to fight Gerald. And still only he and his girlfriend knew their terrible secret. Soon, everyone would know something was wrong.

Parks went into training camp at Fort Pierce, Florida, to train for McClellan and had to undergo a regulation medical. He came up HIV positive. One of the officials monitoring the test passed the result on to Lou Duva, mistakenly thinking Parks was a Duva fighter. Duva told *Ring* magazine, who told everybody else in boxing, and the challenger knew this was now getting bad: he'd have to take another test, preferably back in his hometown of Greenville. Moretti claims Parks got a friend to take the test.

It came up negative and Parks convinced Epps he was clean. The big fight was back on. Almost. Marc Ratner, the executive director of the Nevada State Athletic Commission, told the fighter, 'We want you to be tested in Nevada.' Parks stopped training, says Moretti. Soon afterwards, he cried off, claiming an injured shoulder. He never boxed again.

'He calls me now and again,' Epps told me. 'I bump into him every once in a while. He's got a little business where he sprays down vinyl in households. But he looks good, gained a lot of weight, weighs about 220 now. He didn't give boxing up, they cut him off. He couldn't fight no more. I believe he would have won one of the three world championships. I really believe he mighta beaten McClellan. We didn't know he was HIV until ... You know, we had our tickets to go to Las Vegas, we had a contract ... We were to leave on Saturday and we went to Florida to train ... They come back, him and his daddy, and was all disappointed. It was HIV.

'I don't know which one give what to who. But Lamar, he was a rounder. All I know, she was saying he gave it to her. But he says now she had been the one. She was a little old puny girl in the first place ... Nobody really knows who did what. I'm not going to say

Samantha or him. It was just one of them things. They know. And I was a friend of both of them.

'Say, how is Gerald doin?'

Blind. Almost deaf. Broke.

'I'll be darned.'

So McClellan never got to fight Parks. Instead he fought Lamar's victim, Baptist. Unfortunately for Gilbert, it wasn't an understudy part he was prepared for. Before this moderate San Diego opponent, all Gerald's twenty-nine wins had come early, twenty-four of them before round four. He'd worked out his finishing formula to perfection and nobody had been able to resist, except the slicksters Milton and Ward. McClellan's set-up punch was a left to the short ribs, the liver killer, knees bent and shoulder dipped – 'You know when a punch like that gets through there is no answer to it. If it is picture perfect, he'll go down, anybody go down,' Gerald would say. It was the punch he used to put away Jay Bell in Puerto Rico, his first defence. No middleweight has won a title fight quicker: thirty seconds. 'The minute I hit him, I knew it was over. I hit him, took a step backwards and just seen him fall.'

Gerald was so confident, he reckoned he should do the job in three rounds, regardless of the opponent. 'I don't see the fight goin' no more than three rounds,' he told promoters of his engagement against Baptist. 'Three rounds gives me enough time to box, to feel him out, through the guard. You know, three rounds is enough for any fight to go.' By now nobody doubted his ability to knock people out quickly. The only question was what would happen should he come across someone who could take him past three rounds, take him the distance again, like Milton and Ward? I wonder if that thought worried McClellan even then?

Right now that didn't matter. Gerald's biggest fight was not with his opponent but with his trainer. His local newspaper, the *Standard-Journal*, reported that McClellan wanted no more of Manny Steward after this one. It looked like the old Kronk dilemma: too many fighters for one star trainer.

Manny would dress up his non-appearance for the Baptist fight, saying he wanted Willie Brown to get TV exposure, that he didn't think Baptist was much of a threat anyway. Gerald figured, though, that Steward was not paying him enough attention. Or respect. He was not the first fighter to feel that way. Or the last.

The MGM Grand Garden looked pretty full for the main event. If it had been Parks in the other corner, the venue and attendance would have been appropriate. This contest might have been bogus but, as ever, the punters didn't tumble. King, with Tyson still inside, was looking to make the most of Gerald. He called this one 'Global Warfare', which didn't make a lot of sense.

Jimmy Lennon Jr, the ring announcer, told us Baptist went by the *nom de guerre* of 'the Sweet Sensation'. He'd been smart enough in his day, but sweet he was no longer. Gerald had abandoned the gold trunks of the Kronk for his favourite green and the G-Man was announced now as from Freeport, not Detroit. It hardly mattered. He could have got by as Billy No-Name from Timbuktu in his underpants for all the resistance he would meet.

There were other changes. In his corner now were Stan and Donnie, alongside Willie Brown. Gerald had gone back to his roots. He liked Donnie, his first cousin, and Stan was the sort of street-smart guy he was comfortable with. He didn't trust the big boys any more. Sugar Ray had let him down, and now Manny wasn't measuring up. Gerald would sort this boxing business out himself.

'And the first thing, Ferdie, that we notice,' says HBO's mike man, 'is that there is no Emanuel Steward.' With information pouring down the announcer's earpiece now, viewers were informed there had been a split over strategy. Ferdie Pacheco, whose critical faculties were never much, jumps right in, winging it. '[Emanuel] was disappointed at his attitude, not losing weight like he wanted him to. And just his strategy. He doesn't want him to go out there and bomb. He wants him to box.'

At which point Gerald, who had said he wanted the early knock-out, puts Mr Baptist on his bum with a left hook, for no count. Ferdie shuts it. Then a right, and another, a second left and Baptist, gone, takes an eight-count. Gerald continues with his strategy of hitting the other guy really hard, as often as he can. The boxing could be put on hold. Gilbert bounces on his pants at 1.53 of the round, takes another count from Richard Steele. Pacheco, who calls himself the fight doctor, says, 'This is academic.' Another tangle of blows, Baptist slides down McClellan's legs and Steele waves it off. The McClellan strategy seems to have held up OK.

Pacheco now decides, 'As a follow-up to that [Steward's absence], I think it's one of those temporary lovers' spats that happen between managers and fighters. I don't think that Emanuel Steward is in any way out. I think they will make it up.'

It was impossible to see how Pacheco had made this leap of logic, with no knowledge of what was going on between fighter and trainer. It seemed the boxing hierarchy were still not regarding Gerald as the master of his own destiny; they saw him as the boxer who was delivered by one of their regular suppliers, in this case Steward's Kronk camp. Gerald didn't see it that way. And what was to come would significantly affect the rest of his career.

Bobby Czyz, boxer turned interviewer, spoke to Steward, who tried to cool rumours of a bust-up. 'I been so busy with other fights and I didn't really have the time to train him. I didn't think that this particular fight was going to be that difficult. I'm with Gerald as a manager. Next time I might have time to train him, fine. You always going to have dissension when you got a big stable of fighters. He's been training eight weeks and I didn't have that kinda time to spend with him in Las Vegas.'

Manny was more concerned at that time with his favourite, Tommy Hearns, and setting up a fight between him and interviewer Czyz, who was still a rated fighter. In the Steward set-up, Gerald was getting shuffled behind a fast-fading Hearns and the less than dynamic WBO light-heavyweight champion Leonzer Barber. 'But the main fight I'm workin' on is Tommy fightin' you,' Steward told Czyz. Not the rematch between Gerald and Jackson on 7 May? No big split, reckoned the Showtime ringside guy, Steve Albert.

Gerald didn't see it so amicably when interviewed in centre ring. King wrapped an arm around the G-Man, like a farmer petting his prize bull. 'I trained the hardest I ever trained,' said McClellan, 'seven and a half weeks. Everybody thought I had a problem makin' weight, but I got it off, like, two weeks ago, real easy. I felt real good out there, strong. And thanks to my man right here, Willie Brown, for stickin' with me, puttin' up with my attitude for the whole time.'

Asked about Steward – or rather informed by Pacheco that Manny says they're still manager and fighter, still friends – Gerald held it together. 'Well, I'm not gonna say nothin' about that. Emanuel know what he did. I'm not gonna criticise nobody on national television, you know, coz I'm a better man than that. But, you know, if it's up to Emanuel, we work something out, and I keep doin' what I did tonight.'

Gilbert Baptist, a nice man by everyone's account, went back to being a probation officer in San Diego.

McClellan, meanwhile, was eager for a challenge. He told King, 'I'm ready now for Julian Jackson, anyone out there – James Toney, Roy Jones, all the big-name guys – coz my name's big too. So I think we can do a big pay day get-together.'

Which brings us on to Jackson–McClellan II, live pay-per-view in Las Vegas, 7 May 1994, almost a year to the day after their first meeting, on a night of rematches, featuring four world-title fights. This time, back in the MGM Garden, Showtime noticed that Steward was not there. They'd split. But they were still describing Gerald as from under Manny's wing, guided now by Willie Brown. Steward and Davimos, meanwhile, were consulting their lawyers. They were going to get some money out of Gerald. McClellan was mixing with what passed for boxing's royalty. It was no more than he deserved. He was as good as any of them. Better. Better than Jackson, certainly. On average, Gerald was spending less than nine minutes on each of his opponents; Jackson's career average was closer to twelve.

Jackson, his sight suspect and his chin findable, had said of McClellan after the first fight, 'Until he came on the scene, he was unknown to us. But I knew he was a very tough fighter and I saw him live in Mexico. He was straight up, and I thought, man, I'm going to take this guy.' But a minute into that first fight, Gerald was on him. 'To my surprise,' Jackson said later, 'he didn't stand straight up. He moved back, and my punches were just a little short as he was stepping back. And that's somethin' that threw me off.'

Jackson reckoned he'd been dreaming about the rematch every

night since the first fight. Sweet dreams. He saw it as his chance to give McClellan a boxing lesson, 'to show the world a side of Julian Jackson they haven't seen'. Like the soles of his boots, as it turned out.

The G-Man staggered Jackson with an overhand right twenty seconds into the fight. The Virgin Islander, so confident beforehand, retreated. McClellan unleashed a hail of unanswered punches and knocked Jackson down. After taking an eight-count, Jackson only had time to move across the ring before McClellan was on him again. He finished him with his trademark punch, the left hook to the body, and the ex-champ was bent double on the floor. Just as Joe Cortez's count reached ten, Jackson made a late gesture to get back on his feet, as beaten champions often do. It had taken Gerald McClellan just one minute and twenty seconds to rid the middleweight division of the most dangerous single-shot puncher it had seen since Tommy Hearns had passed through it. He unleashed a tempest of hurt and Jackson, brave man, went to the ropes, put his gloves around his ears and drowned in his own pained confusion.

It was McClellan's third straight first-round knockout. He was 31–2 with twenty-nine early wins. He got $250,000 – $75,000 more than the washed-up Jackson – and he was looking for a lot more now. So was everyone else. For King and Showtime, and anyone else hanging on, McClellan was the next meal ticket outside the heavyweights. Jackson's day was over and Gerald had slotted into his place. This is boxing's way, a carousel of mislaid baggage.

And McClellan, pumped from braining Julian in one, said after disposing of him, 'I'm the hardest puncher in boxin' and whoever I hit gonna lay down.'

Then he reveals something about himself that would have a bearing on what was left of his career. '. . . [Jackson]'s been in the ring so long, he being a veteran . . . If it were me, with the experience I got, I'd go down on one knee, get the heat off of me, get my mind together and collect myself and get up and start all over again.'

That's what Sayers did against Heenan, for more than two hours. Taking the knee. Coming back up to scratch. And that's what

Gerald cools his head with a blast of water during training in London. © Vanessa Winship.

Gerald did, once before, in his first fight with Jackson twelve months earlier, when Julian hit him low. Champions always get up.

The sooner the better. The code. The standard boxing lie. Don't let the other guy think you're hurt. As Gerald said, he was smarter than Todd. He reckoned the smart fighter beats the physical fighter every time. Gerald was smart and physical. Also, he had an aura about him now. He was 'bad'.

'This is my last fight at middleweight,' McClellan said. 'I'm moving up to super middleweight. Nobody can beat me.'

Only one fighter would get that opportunity.

5

Round Three *Fighters and Writers*

Steve Albert: 'Round two was a good one for Benn, after almost being counted out in round one . . .'

Ferdie Pacheco: 'Nobody's ever questioned Benn's courage or his desire to fight, that's one thing . . . but we don't know what will happen when McClellan . . . oh, boy! Nice uppercut by Benn!'

Albert: 'A right uppercut by Benn! A right hand! An uppercut! A wild miss by McClellan . . .'

Pacheco: 'Benn's a little bit anxious now. He almost feels like he's got this guy on the run . . .'

Albert: 'This isn't a fight. It's a Hollywood script!'

Pacheco: 'It's McClellan who's got the power. It remains to be seen if he's got the heart to stay in there . . . Right now McClellan's still in the recovery stage. He's lettin' the other guy burn himself out.'

McClellan goes southpaw. Misses. Misses. Misses. Something's wrong. And then . . .

Ferdie: 'A hard right by McClellan! And that staggers Benn.'

It does. He's suffering. Twenty seconds to go. Nigel swings, misses but, as Albert says, 'He's hanging in there.'

Down in the orchestra pit of opinions, soft, well-paid fingers move to the beat of the fight. Jabbing on to virgin paper, they make a communal dig at a familiar drama. Or skimming a laptop keyboard, at a radio mike, embroidering the TV pictures with suitably dramatic words, snapping a picture. How many ways to describe a punch? Blow, bludgeon, bang, wing, hit, hurt, hack, thump, thrash, hook, jab, cross, uppercut, stick, belt . . .

The press seats used to be peopled by old guys in hats. A cigar, sometimes. Some of them had given the canvas the pleasure of an odd visit themselves, standing up or horizontally. There's a few left

– hatless and cigar-free now – but the sport's shrinking and, along with it, the press coverage. There used to be regulars ringside at York Hall in Bethnal Green – local-paper guys of good vintage chronicling boxing's underbelly. There used to be regulars from the nationals, designated boxing writers, and, while there are still a swag of former world champions with press credentials, good judges and good blokes, there are not many full-timers assigned by the national newspapers to write exclusively about boxing any more. A lot of writers-at-large, who go to 'the big ones', mind you. Boxing has become an add-on for the sports pages.

When Srikumar Sen retired as the boxing correspondent of *The Times* early in 2001 to spend more time with his furniture collection in North Wales, he went without regret. He sees the marginalisation of what was a mainstream sport. Once, either side of the last war, there were as many as 40,000 pros working in Britain. Now there are probably 10,000 throughout the world. And fewer than 700 in Britain. Same in the amateurs, although recent years have seen something of a revival. There are an estimated 4,000 senior amateurs in Britain today.

When boxing was in nearly every school, in every borough, the Amateur Boxing Association championships attracted huge audiences. The BBC televised the tournament, live, from the regional semi-final stages. There were no headguards and the audience knew and identified with the boxers. It made stars out of them. That coverage has dwindled to highlights of the finals.

There is hope. When Greg Dyke took over as the corporation's Director-General in 2000, he inherited a near-bare cupboard. As a man whose first job in journalism was as a freelance boxing writer, he turned to the pugilists for help. He signed the Olympic super-heavyweight gold medallist Audley Harrison, then the world heavyweight champion Lennox Lewis, as well as – unsuccessfully – going after the signature of the world's then best featherweight, Naseem Hamed. Just as well. Hamed lost. But so did Lewis. And Harrison, meanwhile, embarked on a professional career whose early stages worryingly resembled the soft days of Frank Bruno on the BBC.

With less enthusiasm, the BBC committed itself to covering the amateurs again, but cherry-picking the best events rather than investing in the grass roots. We were still a long way from the old days when boxing was automatically at the top table of sport.

Sky, meanwhile, had done a fine job of sustaining boxing – but for a reduced audience and a higher price. Now it had the BBC at its side and it was time to see if boxing could get up and punch its way back into the hearts of the public. By the time this book is being read we'll know whether those efforts were successful and boxing has been dragged away from the edge of a serious downturn. Maybe we'll get our boxing correspondents back one day.

The night of the fight, ITV held the cameras. It was their penultimate bout before they walked away from boxing for several years. There would be big shifts in the sport's politics, big changes in financing. The few would be much better paid, but seen less. The tribe of under-card boxers would get more work, but would walk around their own streets unrecognised. The writers, meanwhile, tried to fill the vacuum as best they could.

Harry – H, as we called him – sat a few seats away. He'd seen it all, from the days he'd pulled the gloves on in his youth back in Portstewart, Northern Ireland, to the moment he realised, then sustained, his dream of travelling the world chronicling the deeds of fighters of all shapes and abilities.

He was shaking his white-mopped head, still wondering about that count in round one. It wasn't just professional diligence. The unspoken shout was this: if Nigel had been counted out in the first, if Newbon hadn't pushed Benn back in the ring, if McClellan had been declared the new world super-middleweight champion there and then, we'd be packing up soon, knocking out a thou to copytakers, then making for the pub for a quick one, or, in Mr Mullan's case, the nearest curry house for a long one. Even now, he asked: 'Curry later?'

Harry's gift was as a writer, a skill which he inherited from his father. For the best part of twenty years, H edited *Boxing News*, the sport's oldest printed friend – 'every fight, every punch, every week' – as well as writing books, newspaper articles, talking on radio and television and generally enhancing our lives with his irrepressible enthusiasm for boxing and boxers.

He maintained it was the only sort of journalism he could do. He wasn't quite the one-trick pony he professed to be, but certainly his relationship with boxing was that of a happy addict. He was my kind of Fight Writer.

'From Homer to Hazlitt . . . from Athens to Zaire, we seem irresistibly drawn to these combats,' wrote Budd Schulberg. Most reckon it started with Pierce Egan, besotted and quirky. Then there was Byron, Thackeray, Dickens, Shaw and others, educated outsiders. The post-Romantics followed: Jack London, A. J. Liebling, Damon Runyon, Ring Lardner, Ernest Hemingway, Jimmy Baldwin, Ben Hecht, William Saroyan, Nelson Algren . . . and on to Mailer, Plimpton, Hamill, Hauser, Joyce Carol Oates (bedazzled intellectuals), as well as the brilliantly unreliable Hunter S. Thompson.

Few fed so feverishly on the fight game as did Liebling. Like many of the others, he did little to dispel the myths. He created many of them, in Rockwellian schmaltz, a witness at a succession of tragedies. Liebling called his minor masterpiece *The Sweet Science*, in echo of Egan, with whose casual dedication in the first 'Boxiana' in 1813 the gifted American dreamer apparently had no argument:

> To those, Sir, who prefer effeminacy to hardihood – assumed refinement to rough Nature – and whom a shower of rain can terrify, under the alarm of their polite frames, suffering from the unruly elements – or would not mind Pugilism, if boxing was not so shockingly vulgar – the following work can create no interest whatever; but to those persons who feel that Englishmen are not automatons . . . *Boxiana* will convey amusement, if not information . . .

The Fight Writers who feasted on this overblown guff sentimentalised their deadly sport. In books, newspaper columns and movie scripts, they indulged themselves in semi-detached machismo. Like war correspondents, they got as close as they could without bleeding. Some, such as Liebling and Plimpton, real ring-war junkies, did spar with ex-champions, aspiring to give a bruised substance to their obsession. But these were literary stunts that demeaned the real thing.

You sometimes have to get away from your own beat for perspective. When Evander Holyfield fought John Ruiz in 2000, the *San Francisco Bay Guardian* sent a writer called Summer Burkes to Vegas to look at the Fight Writers. Summer was confused.

'The boys at the press table,' he wrote, 'seem surprised when I propose that live boxing matches are as weirdly erotic as watching a football game or a male rock and roll band, since (among other things) it's one of the only ways that men are socially encouraged to be physically close to each other.'

Burkes asked them why they liked it. A writer from a boxing web site told him boxing was 'comic books come to life'. He liked the boxers' 'superhuman strength, speed and agility'. Not to mention the stories.

The writer from San Francisco was fascinated by the morbidity of it, the fact that fighters could die in the ring.

No one wanted to fight himself. 'None of us could take even one punch,' said web guy.

Since *Fight Club* was published, in 1996, some very strange things have been happening to those males who like the idea of 'once-removed violence'. All of a sudden, seduced by good literature and a not bad film of the book, they fancy a little go themselves. Or they say they do. On message boards all over the Internet, thousands of cyber-fighters issue empty challenges to other addicts. If even a small proportion of them want to go through with their boasts, that's a lot of broken bones. A lot of health risk. A lot of testosterone.

So I went to talk to Chuck Palahniuk, who wrote *Fight Club*. His baby had grown into a mini-monster, from an obscure book to a blockbuster movie to a cult – but he was OK with it. He liked Susan Faludi's book, *Stiffed*, in which she talks about male emasculation. He is jealous. If a man were to write that, he says, he'd be called a whining wimp. But he reckons women recognise that men have been de-balled in modern times and are now unsure how, when, where or why to throw the next punch. Or at whom. Growing up in Portland, Chuck threw punches indiscriminately in bars all over town. His friends tired of his self-indulgence. But Chuck felt more alive than he had ever done.

He doesn't fight now. He's fortyish and rich. But he's glad he did. He reckons men who have never fought will be for ever jealous of him too.

We talk writing and fighting and fathers for an hour or so. Chuck is big on this 'father thing'. He thinks they should be training up our caveman side a bit more. I'm not sure. My own father boxed a little in the army, but you'd never meet a gentler man. He didn't need to tell me or my two brothers about being 'men'. No need to shout. Once, while training to kill for King and country at Aldershot in 1943, Dad boxed a round with a visiting American GI called Joe Louis. But he'd never told me that until a couple of years ago. And, strange as it may seem, I never felt the urge to go out and wreck a bar because he never taught me how to throw a left hook. I wasn't sure what Chuck was on about.

'No matter how well we were trained by our fathers,' Palahniuk says, 'we started to make that leap ourselves. There's something in all this examination of men's cultures that says fathers can't do this. And one archetype that is held up is the boxing trainer. The boxing trainer, or the drill sergeant or the coach takes over after the father, he completes the job that the father can't complete, because he's just too close to the fighter. It's funny, because I see all these grizzled old boxing coaches, and they're like sixty or seventy years old, and they really are archetype. They're immensely important to the guys that they train – and to the women that they train too.'

Burgess Meredith types?

'Exactly. And they're not really fathers at all. They take over after a father.'

That might be it. Chuck's American. He seizes on the movie image instantly. Burgess Meredith. I wasn't serious, but he was. That afternoon, he'd heard about a real-life phenomenon in Brazil, funk balls. These are disco-driven nights of violence in clubs in the shanty towns of Brazil. I'd heard of them too. But I'd also heard kids die in these fights. As many as sixty in one year. Chuck, initially fascinated, is suddenly appalled.

'They die? And there's, like guys on the floor, and they run between these lines, right, fighting. Why do people do that?'

Tell me, Chuck. You're the guy who wrote *Fight Club*. But then, like the A-Team, people don't die in *Fight Club*. It's just a story, right?

Chuck, I was glad to hear, had not grown up a dysfunctional misfit looking for a way to put a hole in his face.

'No, I was told the whole time to walk away, run away, turn the other cheek. So I spent my adolescence and all through college avoiding it and thinking it was entirely valueless and stupid and pointless and self-destructive and blah-blah-blah . . . And at the same time I was following a very set-down pattern for success, established by my blue-collar parents. Which was hard work, go to school, be productive and create things and I really probably wasn't going any further than my parents were. To build something, to contribute . . . not realising that a little bit of destruction would allow me to create so much more. In a way it was tearing down myself, as a precursor to creating myself in a much bigger, better way. I did get to a point where this whole blueprint wasn't working for me and I went through a period when I was in a lot of fights and I really started to enjoy them.'

Did you know why?

'It was this huge suppressed frustration that my life wasn't turning out and I was doing everything I was supposed to do and it still wasn't turning out. At a flashpoint, things would happen and I would end up in a fight with someone. It was a little bit of an act of resignation because I felt I had nothing to lose at that point.'

I liked Chuck. But I reckoned he thought too much.

Tim Lott, a British writer also fascinated by violence, saw *Fight Club* and *Stiffed* this way when he reviewed them in tandem for the *Daily Telegraph* in 1999: 'What men are missing nowadays, the film seems to say, is the opportunity to beat one another senseless.'

He goes on:

Reading about this film brought back to me a vivid, true-life image: an image of a man – an ordinary, liberal family man – standing on his feet baying for the blood of another man who was being beaten almost to death. I was that man. The event was a boxing match: Nigel Benn vs Gerald McClellan, London Docklands Arena, 1995.

It was his first fight. He was scared of his emotions, of what might happen inside him if 'the bout turned too ugly'.

What, I wondered, was 'too ugly'?

As blow after blow rained on the hapless McClellan, as the coating of blood on the American's face thickened, and the crowd turned into a single, baying mass of rage and excitement and lust for violence, I found myself on my feet, red-faced, in full sweat, screaming. Screaming, in truth, for McClellan's hide, for McClellan's absolute destruction. I was either not myself or, perhaps, I was more myself than I had ever been in my life.

There was no 'coating of blood'. But for Lott, the myth and the false memory were stronger than the truth. As if the truth weren't bad enough.

Inevitably, Hollywood found out about boxing. One of the first pieces of moving film was of a fight. The twenty-foot ring, it seemed, was made for the camera. Of the six hundred or so movies about sport in the twentieth century, boxing comprised by far the biggest genre, providing nearly 140 efforts of various quality. With few exceptions, the story was sad. From *The Harder They Fall* to *Fat City*. From *The Set-Up* to *Raging Bull*. From *Kid Galahad* (1937) to *Kid Galahad* (1962). From *Rocky I* to *Rocky V*. Or is it *VI*?

The most idiosyncratic of them, my favourite, is Robert Wise's *The Set-Up*, made in 1949 when the Mob ruled. In it, Robert Ryan's Bill 'Stoker' Thompson fights in a place called Dreamland. A blind man rages in the crowd. Across the street, Stoker's girl waits in a room in the Cosy Hotel. Stoker defies the fix that has been paid for, and afterwards gets his hands mangled in an alleyway by the guy he's double-crossed. Based on a long narrative poem by the jazz-age Bohemian, Joseph Moncure March, the film occupies real time, seventy-two minutes. Classic theatre. It encapsulates boxing. The fact that Ryan boxed for four years at Dartmouth (not badly, by all accounts) and thereby added athletic authenticity to the deal, saved it from being *Rocky*. This was a poem of a fight. A poem of a fight movie.

In 1975, Wise told some students at a seminar how he'd hung around a run-down part of Long Beach to research the film. He watched real boxing people then got actors to recreate what he saw. He also watched the audiences.

'A lot of the business in audience reactions is from there,' he told them. 'The fellow with the radio I saw at the Hollywood Legion, same with the guy with the cigar and the fat man. The blind man may seem far-fetched to you but he was an actual character in San Francisco that Art Cohn used to see regularly every Friday night at the fights. He'd come with his buddy and have him describe what was going on.'

Generally, though, the marketing of street glamour distorts reality in the very act of reaching for it. The fictional representation of boxing has to be dramatic. Even the fighters fall for it.

Lurching between self-parody and another prison term, Mike Tyson was as much a creation of the Fight Writers as he was of his first guru, Cus D'Amato, or Don King, of the streets of Brownsville, the strip clubs of Las Vegas or the rap clubs of south Chicago.

Tyson, as near a throwback to James Figg and the bareknuckle boys as we have seen since Sonny Liston, was tutored in the traditions of the fight business by the late Jim Jacobs, a patrician and rather dull boxing obsessive who owned a priceless library of old films. Packaged as *Greatest Fights of the Century*, that archive introduced a lot of post-war TV kids to boxing's past. I remember devouring episodes of it when I was growing up in Australia – it was introduced every Saturday by an old fight face called Ray Mitchell. Ray knew everything there was to know about boxing. After a while, I thought I did too. But I knew what I liked. And I liked *Greatest Fights of the Century*. So did Mike, apparently. Those old films, in their original form as shown to him by Jim Jacobs, were to have a profound effect on the young Tyson. He was fascinated by the flickering, stick-figure fighters, their hard, lean bodies pummelled in and out of semi-consciousness on grainy old film.

No contemporary boxer empathises with the image of fighter as predator-cum-victim like Tyson does. It's why his hero is Liston, whose grave near McCarron Airport in Las Vegas he visits regularly. Originally, Mike bought the whole thing. He knew about Sayers and Heenan and the others. Jacobs lectured him about the tradition of boxing, told him that tradition started in England. Bare-fisted. Tyson loved that. It gave lustre to his discredited ghetto upbringing, it made him 'respectable' because of the nobility and history attached to what otherwise would get you five to ten.

Tyson recognised that a large part of that integrity relied on a fighter's courage, his willingness to go to war. That's what he signed up for. Yet, when Tyson faced his own examinations, his own real ring world, doubts crowded in on him. Buster Douglas battered Mike in Tokyo and, as he scrambled about on the canvas for his mouthpiece, an inner voice told him to get up. He didn't beat the count. But he tried. Mike had been well tutored. Then later, when softened by time, drink, pills and transitory friends, Tyson did not respond so instinctively. When he turned away as Evander Holyfield forced his standing resignation near the end of their first encounter, rescued by the referee, Iron Mike discovered he was not the caveman Bob Fitzsimmons thought every fighter should be. Fitz wrote to *The Ring* magazine in 1914 complaining about the soft fighters of the day. Soon enough, they would be called to arms of a deadlier kind.

We've had our bareknuckled time on the edge in Britain. Enough with the brutality. Now we're fat and soft, a bit smarter. Americans? They're still addicted. They have Extreme This and Extreme That. They go to make-believe wrestling, know it's rigged, and then pretend it's not. Or do they pretend to pretend? They go to see *Fight Club*, a movie of a novel – and then, missing the point, they start their own. I spoke to an interesting man from Sunnyside, south Chicago, called Pat 'Big Lew' Lewandowski.

Pat kept telling me he was bald and weighed 330 pounds and how heavyweights are whores. 'Not worth a fuckin' nickel.' He promoted, but, 'You know, how ya make a dollar in baahxin' any more?' Pat's got a sideline. He runs something called *Fite Klub*. He swears it's not 'ultimate' fighting. He described it to the authorities who closed him down as 'pankration'. I was sure he was aware this was the ancient and very bloody version of fighting practised by the ancient Greeks.

'I don't let my guys hit 'em in the face when they're on the ground,' says Pat. 'I am not feeding Christians to the lions, and there are other people out there who are doing that.'

There certainly are. Pat's old mate is Sean Curtin, who knows Stan Johnson and the boys, regular visitors to Illinois. Sean looks after boxing, among other things, for the State Government and has been lumbered with the surreal title, Chief of General Enforcement for the Illinois Department of Professional Regulation. Droogs, beware. Sean tells me about 'ultimate fighting'. 'These fights, they crop up three or four times a year. There have been a few deaths, guys still in comas.' Sean closed Pat down. Pat sued and lost. Then Pat fell out with his landlord. They closed his gym. Pat is adamant what he is doing is no worse than wrestling. And you can't say fairer than that. Sean's got a tape of one of Pat's shows. 'On the tape, there were no gloves, there was punching and kicking while on their feet and on the ground, which is what we consider ultimate fighting.'

As a body of journalists, the American Fight Writers are a pleasant bunch. Well schooled and diligent, they are as objective as their British counterparts. Mostly. But the audience they direct their prose at are, often, the same punters who will go down a basement and watch middle-class fantasists belt each other senseless. It is a climate of unrestrained masculinity. And, to a man – fighters, writers and readers – they have come to despise quitters. There is no greater crime in American professional boxing. You are less than a man if you quit. A dog.

Any sign of quitting in a headline fighter in America spells the end of his career, more or less. Andrew Golota, the 'crazy Pole from Chicago', as he is generally referred to, has universally been consigned to the spit bucket after quitting against Tyson – in Detroit, of all places. Where Gerald went to learn about professional boxing from Manny and the Kronk. Where the Coventry stylist Errol Christie got mashed in sparring. Where a lot of sheep got separated from a lot of goats.

So no amount of medical evidence produced later showing Golota risked serious injury if he'd carried on against Tyson could soothe the media mob. They made conciliatory noises, but they didn't mean it. They, like the punters, went to that fight between two ring animals wanting a lot of heavy action. That's the way it was sold.

They didn't want pretty. They wanted ugly. In their words, in their papers, on their TV screens. They knew the chances of aberrant behaviour were high. This was a fight, after all, between two heavyweights with widely publicised psychological problems, a fight which television bought, for a pay-per-view audience, because that was the selling point. It was the same company, Showtime, who went ahead with the delayed-tape screening of Benn–McClellan, even when word had got through that Gerald was fighting for his life.

There was no title at stake in Tyson–Golota, just another slice of boxing's credibility as a sport. To deny the real reason for putting it on is to risk derision in any serious discussion about why fist fighting in front of a paying audience exists in the first place. The questions about the state of Golota's head, not to mention Tyson's, should have been asked – and answered – before the event, not after. The conclusion should have been that neither man was fit to share a boxing ring – especially with each other. The blame, if that is what we're looking for, lies with the people who sanctioned and supported the fiasco from its inception to its inevitable and unedifying conclusion.

But TV and the Fight Writers didn't get what they wanted and they couldn't forgive Golota for cheating them. They wanted Sayers–Heenan and they got Laurel and Hardy. It had nothing to do with boxing. This was train-crash fighting, and train-crash journalism.

When a distressed, pissed on, hurt and confused Golota (whose stutter and police record back in Poland told you he was never destined to run for public office) declined to talk to the television interviewer afterwards, Showtime's senior producer of sports and event programming, Jay Larkin, went for him. 'Now! You piece of shit!' the cheated exec screamed at the fighter. And Golota complied, mumbling an incoherent excuse about it not being his night. That he was hurt.

'In my sixteen years of boxing,' Larkin said, 'I've never seen a more blatant act of cowardice. The man is a coward. He does not deserve to be licensed anywhere ever again on this planet. He will never appear on Showtime again.'

The *New York Daily News* headline said it all: 'Golota Hits & Runs Like a True Coward'.

'Hopefully, Golota won't quit anymore,' Mike Katz wrote on the *House of Boxing* web site. 'Hopefully, he won't fight anymore.'

Ron Borges, in the *Boston Globe*, said, 'Then it was over, and so, hopefully, was the career of a sorry excuse for a fighter named Golota.'

Golota had quit before, which annoyed the Fight Writers. He imploded against Michael Grant when in front on points, and twice against Riddick Bowe he got himself disqualified. Neither did he throw a meaningful blow when Lennox Lewis jumped on him in a round.

'Everybody was right to think Golota was a dog and a quitter,' said another American commentator. 'Everybody was right to ask him to go out and fight if all he had was superficial cuts. But he was falling apart inside and we didn't know it. Thank God he quit or we might have had a death on our hands.' The commentator was Dr Pacheco, whose views on quitting wavered in the wind, it appeared.

Elsewhere, the dudgeon was rampant. In a long, emotional piece under the headline 'The Heart of A Fighter Always Beats', a writer called Ted Bodenrader compared Golota's performance to that of a young bantamweight in Boston that night. Bobby Benson, a twenty-six-year-old prospect from Saugus, Massachusetts, was having his fifteenth fight as Bobby Tomasello, his father's fight name. He had fourteen wins and a lot of plans.

Around the same time the Polish heavyweight was colored a very fitting yellow, compliments of the refreshments he was doused with by irate fans as he exited the arena, a young man from Saugus was engaged in the kind of battle that neither Golota nor Tyson could ever even fathom.

It had been Bobby's first fight on TV, for which he earned $5,000, compared with Golota's $2.1 million; Tomasello came to the ring undefeated. At the end of ten tough rounds, his opponent, Steve Dotse from Ghana, was announced as a winner on a majority decision. That was changed to a draw and Tomasello, back in his dressing room drinking a soda, felt pleased enough. They brought him back to the ring to accept the applause of the crowd. He returned to the dressing room and collapsed. Within minutes, the judges realised they had got it wrong twice. Dotse *was* the actual winner. But, by then, Tomasello was unconscious and on his way to hospital. He died after a short time on a life-support machine. And he died, in his own mind, an unbeaten fighter.

The Fight Writers were at least happy with that.

Even winners got it in the neck. Lennox Lewis, for instance, when he beat Holyfield in their second fight. According to Borges, Lewis was his idea of an 'imitation of a fighter'. This is an interesting way to put it. He'd said the same about Golota. Borges likes 'real fighters' but what he regards as reality does not correspond with my dictionary understanding of the word.

Because boxing itself is an imitation of fighting. If it were real, if it were not a representation of something much more sinister, we would be witnessing the finish fights of old, where a man was beaten only when he surrendered (to be derided until he died), when he was incapable of standing, or seeing even. Men like Greb, Langford, Broughton. Like Sayers and Heenan. If real fighting had not evolved into pseudo-fighting (albeit still highly dangerous), we would not be watching contests where arbitrarily applied rules were brought into play by a third party. We would be watching men trying to kill each other. This is the language of boxing. Mancini, who is not one of those bloodthirsty types, says of Benn–McClellan, 'Never before in all my years in boxing did I see two guys go out there trying to kill each other like those two did that night.' He did not mean 'kill' in the literal sense. But pretty close to it. Modern 'fighting' has been cleansed of the one element that makes it truly primal: the unequivocal, unnegotiable hurtle towards death. But tell that to the heroes with notebooks.

Fighters themselves still have to talk the macho talk, to give the Fight Writers their quotes. Quotes that sell fights for promoters. Quotes that Harry, for one, would not buy.

American fighters often talk about 'killing the other guy'. It is accepted rhetoric. It raises the temperature, gets the turnstiles moving. David Tua, characterised as a Samoan warrior by the media and himself before he fought Lewis, knows the language: 'It is instinct, inner strength,' he says. 'I am a warrior by nature, by birth. It's my destiny to be a warrior. I was born from a family of warriors, my people were always warriors. Once you have the warrior in your blood, it doesn't go away.'

In echo of McClellan, he concludes, 'In the ring, once you go to war, you go to war.'

If Tua did not talk like this, he couldn't function as a fighter, because he has no other role. He is not pretty, he doesn't dance. He rumbles. And, up until he met the consummate boxer in Lewis, he did so with pleasing, ticket-selling effectiveness. Once beaten, the Fight Writers turned on him. He was a dog.

Lewis, the heavyweight so derided by Borges, not only beat Holyfield, the heavyweight so admired by Ron and his colleagues (and quite rightly), but he made the lightest work of the Samoan warrior. As with all great ring executioners, he cuts short the challenge of inadequates. With little or no collateral damage. Hit and don't be hit.

It took Lewis a decade to be taken seriously. He was too polite, didn't talk dirty. They even whispered he was gay. And, so relaxed was he about the accusation, he couldn't get mad. That did it for some of the guys. If someone calls you a faggot, you at least ought to be very, very angry. As he matured, the champ got a bit bored with some of the carping. He started standing people up, getting to press conferences late. Just like Tyson. A heavyweight with attitude: wasn't that what they wanted?

Before Lewis defended his title against the South African

McClellan had a superb body for boxing – muscled and loose at the top, tapering to slim, light legs. But he worked for it. Here in the gym in London, he tones his neck and stomach. © *Vanessa Winship.*

François Botha in London, he shared his irritation about this stereotyping: 'Every fight there's always some kind of rhetoric that goes on, some kind of issue. The first fight with Holyfield, everyone was saying that Lennox Lewis doesn't have heart; the second fight was, you know, robbery. I'm a boxer. And I'm the best heavyweight boxer in the world.'

Lewis nearly always calls himself a boxer. Not a fighter. So, you can imagine the unspoken glee of the Fight Writers when Hasim 'the Rock' Rahman knocked out the champion in Johannesburg in April 2001.

'H' wasn't around for that one. He died of cancer a couple of years before. Yet, right to the end, he did not lose his enthusiasm for boxing and all its ups and downs. He took it as he found it. Harry was an interpreter, not a disseminator, of nonsense. And he had a heightened appreciation of the ridiculous. He found dignity in the endeavour of the combatants, but rarely in the cleverness of the people who paid them. He particularly did not take to the representation of fighters as pawns, foolish and disposable. Sometimes, he also failed to see how devious fighters could be. If there were a university degree in lying – let's call it the art of deception – you'd find all the professors you wanted down the gym. Harry would usually give the fighter the benefit of the doubt.

Not long before he quit life, in awful pain, we were sitting in his hotel room way past midnight. It was a few hours after he'd covered his last fight, Joe Calzaghe successfully defending his WBO super-middleweight title against Robin Reid in Newcastle, and Harry was reminiscing. He'd been very lucky, he said, to have the opportunity to get so close to a sport he loved. The money wasn't always brilliant but, as often as not, we were getting paid better than the fighters. He hoped he'd not made too many mistakes in his boxing writing, that he'd been fair and honest. I told him he'd been more than that. Nobody was respected more in our business, I said.

Harry knew this was it, though. He had a few months left and had carried on working for as long as he could stand the pain. Soon he would have to go off to hospital to die. I lit up a spliff and Harry's eyes twinkled through the bloodshot. He'd been offered a trip to Cuba, but couldn't take it, he said. That would have been a trip to boxing heaven, mixing with Teofilo Stevenson, Felix Savon, maybe even meeting Fidel. 'But then again,' he said, 'I've seen Ali. You can have too much of a good thing in this life.'

Watt: 'Who would have thought in the first round that Benn would have McClellan backing off in the third? Suddenly McClellan has to concentrate on defence.'

Gutteridge: 'These first-round wins McClellan's had, it's as if nothing succeeds like success. He's got overconfident.'

Nevertheless, a long right shakes Benn. McClellan is still dangerous. Still hurting and, with single shots at least, hurting maybe more than Benn. But Nigel is doubling up, and rumbling forward every second. The last time he went backwards was when he went through the ropes. It is the champion who is dictating the rhythm of the fight. And that, as Sugar Ray Robinson often said, is where fights are won and lost.

Gutteridge: 'He's hurting all right, but he's come back a lot better in this round, Benn.'

6

Round Four *Ambrose in Wonderland*

Albert: 'Showing an amazing amount of guts, Nigel Benn ... He has stormed back with a tremendous heart ... You gotta wonder what's going through the mind of McClellan right now; he thought he had him.'

Pacheco: 'McClellan's waiting too long, letting the other guy get started ... He almost got an easy knockout. But he got out of his game plan. He got into a fist fight instead of a boxing match.'

Albert: 'McClellan, who usually fights as if he's double-parked ... his last three fights, first-round knockouts. The question is, if this goes on and on, it's Benn who's gone the distance ... McClellan, rocked with a left hook there!'

Pacheco: 'Sometimes he looks too confused when he gets hit by a hard hand ... fighting like he's got cobwebs in his head ...'

The pace has been set at fast-medium. Benn looks as if he thinks he can finish it, with bar-room swings of minimal subtlety and maximum meanness. Asaro warns Benn for holding and hitting. Daft.

Benn's work loses shape, he lunges with a right. McClellan has slowed; catches some of Benn's clumsier punches. Benn's concentration is slipping. Gerald's mouthpiece almost permanently at the front of his lips; his focus has gone. Takes a good right, hangs on. He's distressed, weary, sucking for air. Benn knocks him sideways, they clinch.

Gerald's previous three fights lasted a total of three minutes; he has not been this deep into a straight-up fist fight since he beat Jackson in 1993. Nigel wobbles him with a left hook, then a chopping right. Gerald still blinking. Paws at his eyes, fiddles with his mouthguard. Benn gets through with full-force headshots. Gerald goes to the waist, hangs on. Unsteady, ready to be taken. Half a minute to go ... His rights are telegraphed, half-hearted. Benn hits him on the back of the head in a clinch. Gerald grimaces. He backs off, goes behind his gloves, peeking through to spot the next attack. Lands a little uppercut at the end, but Benn is on fire.

Pacheco: 'What a fight this is, and what a crowd. These people are goin' crazy here.'

Albert: 'Nigel Benn has taken away the ferocious ring presence of Gerald McClellan.'

There have been many colourful characters in Nigel Benn's life. Those that we know about have entertained us royally on occasions with their outrageousness. Benn has enjoyed them too, up to a point. But he has dismissed them as quickly as he has embraced them if he reckoned they had abused his trust and friendship. Two of the most interesting are Ambrose Mendy and Peter DeFreitas . . .

Benn had made a spectacular start in the fight game, a year before McClellan got going as a pro. Before Jones too. In south London on 28 January 1987, he stopped Graeme Ahmed in two brutal rounds. Nobody was surprised. Benn had introduced himself to the paying public with an ad in *Boxing News* proclaiming his credentials, and his first trainer, Brian Lynch, did a splendid job in shaping this time bomb into an explosion. He hardly ever sparred, concentrating instead on getting his army-trained body into fighting condition. Benn, his street energy diverted to the ring, thrived on the regime.

Boxing once a month until Christmas, he knocked out or stopped another eleven selected opponents in a total of twenty-two rounds. Where his early education differed from Gerald's was in the slow ratcheting-up of quality coming out of the other corner, most significantly in the American Reggie Miller, who made him work for seven rounds before succumbing at the Royal Albert Hall on 2 December.

Benn would learn from that bout and go another ten fights undefeated – before running into the determined Michael Watson on a wild night at Finsbury Park in May 1989. In a crossing of learning curves, that was about the time McClellan was losing his first fight as well. It would be six years before they met, each accumulating titles and knowledge that they hoped, when it came to it, would get them through the sort of horror that is always possible in the ring.

I suspect Benn's education was more thorough. He'd had to get off the floor to beat Anthony Logan in 1988, and he got over his Watson setback by rebuilding his career in the United States. That was a bold move, but typical of a fighter who loved to push himself to the limit. It was that period of his career, I believe, in which Benn put the miles on the clock that got him through his fight with McClellan.

It is worth dwelling, though, on the Watson fight. In keeping with the carnival atmosphere, it was held in a tent. This was not the only ludicrous aspect of the occasion. There are plenty of bizarre excuses in the annals of boxing, but Benn topped them in this one. Floored by a jab in the sixth, he couldn't beat the count – and later said his new hairstyle contributed to his discomfort throughout the fight. This is the only recorded instance of a boxer blaming his hairdresser for losing a fight.

Mendy, no stranger to the bizarre, remembers it as an emotional and sad affair. Benn, who would fall out with Mendy before long, would not disagree.

I met Ambrose soon after he got out of jail for, I think, the fifth time. If it was only the fourth, I apologise. I would not want to damage a man's reputation unnecessarily. Especially someone whose ambition was to be the next Don King.

We met at a restaurant in central London. I paid. Jane Bown, the peerless portrait photographer, took the pictures. She reckoned Ambrose had a face with a million stories. I told her that had to be a conservative estimate. After turning up an hour late (way past fashionable), Ambrose settled down to seduce the tape recorder.

'The truth of the matter is that Nigel Benn the boxer was a great, great fighter; he should have been an all-time great. Nigel Benn should have been up there with anyone you care to mention in the middleweight division. He was a natural middleweight but he proved that a leopard can change its spots, from a walk-in wrecking machine, following the defeat against Michael Watson, when he wanted to quit – and I do think that in the fight itself Nigel quit, he wasn't knocked out. I know that better than anybody else, I'm the guy that walked with him [to and from the ring].'

But you weren't licensed to be a second, were you?

'I wasn't physically in his corner, but I was Nigel's mentor, manager, agent, best friend – and, in the fight itself, he just gave up on himself.'

It's hard to judge how significant this experience would be, come 25 February 1995. But it seems Benn had done his resignation bit, against Watson. Once was enough. It wasn't, to use the cruel argot of the trade, a 'swallow', because Benn had given it everything. It was just that he had no more to give.

'When Nigel was on the floor,' Mendy went on, 'he sort of came to his senses, common sense, and got up, and you can actually see Nigel standing behind the referee as the referee counts "nine". It may have been a blessing in disguise. But I do know that when we got back to the changing rooms, there were tears, crying, you know. He's saying "It's all gone, it's all gone" ...'

Busted up in front of his supporters and listening to a fortune disappear with every toll of the referee's count, Benn's life could get no lower. For the time being.

'He thought he'd lost everything. Because of the hype – Nigel believed in all the hype. He really believed he was going to blow Michael Watson away. Nigel underestimated, grossly under-estimated, Michael Watson and it's outrageous that he blames the corner [for his defeat] ...'

Nigel talks about having spent several hours braiding his hair before the fight ...

'Yeah, but that was his choice. And before every fight there was a woman situation. You know, he was a tremendous womaniser. But that's not uncommon for boxers. But I don't know how emo-tionally committed he was to those relationships.'

A very emotional man.

'Very.'

Were you close?

'Absolutely. There's no question that Nigel regarded me as a brother, as a dad. We were as close as the join you can't see in the table. One of the things I'm asked every day of my life is: what happened, why did you break up? Well, when Nigel hit a crisis point I was always there. I could pre-empt what was going to happen. I prepared best-case scenarios, and worst-case scenarios. But, more importantly, what I brought to Nigel was a marketing machine. You know, I recognised that Nigel Benn, the property, had a life cycle. We knew that with our approach we had to differentiate, there were markets, there were possibilities of reinvention, reinstatement, and that was what Nigel was able to do, clearly: to reinstate himself.'

I was starting to drown in Ambrosia. Mendy has a gift for making nonsense sound plausible.

'In the dressing room, to give you an example, amidst all this [after losing to Watson], I asked Nigel a question, when he said . . . and he spoke in the first person . . . "I've mucked everything up, I've done this, I've done that . . ." – he wasn't blaming anybody else. He was talking in truth, you know, crying. And I said to him, "Yeah, that's right, you did it. You fucked up, you didn't listen to Brian [Lynch, his then trainer], you didn't listen to Sharron [his first wife], you wanted to run about with that silly girl. You decided to sit on a floor all night long getting those things in your hair . . ." And at this time he was in agony . . .'

Exactly how long did he take to get his hair braided? He says in the book it was four hours . . .

'Twenty-one hours. That's twenty-one hours. Show that hairdo to an Afro-weaver and he'll tell you, "Four hours? It's impossible." It was ludicrous, but, of course, he was sat in closer proximity to a female and that's where he wanted to be . . . It's a terrible thing . . . But you still can't take away . . . This man had the most focus, he had the most incredible willpower . . .'

Ambrose was getting away from me again.

Back to the dressing room, then. This is how Mendy remembers the rest of a revealing conversation.

'You fucked everything else up, Nige, you wouldn't listen to this, you wouldn't listen to that. Do you still believe?'

'I'm sorry, I'm sorry, I'm sorry. What we goin' to do, Ambrose?'

'Oh yeah, what *we* goin' to do? *We?*'

'Do you still believe you can be champion of the world?'

'Of course I can, of course I do.'

'Right, well get off your fuckin' arse, coz we're goin' back in the ring.'

And they did. It was some re-entry. Watson's fans were going berserk, still. Benn's were subdued and inconsolable. The police, sensing trouble, had earlier declared Finsbury Park a no-go area.

The ring was still surrounded by celebrities, either settling bets or rubbing their heads in wonder. Only those smarter observers, like the *Sun*'s Colin Hart, who'd tipped the result and the round, were unfazed.

And in walked Benn. For the second time.

'We went into the ring and I said to Nigel, "Go over and laud Watson, because this could go off here in a terrible, terrible way." And he went over and he said – and it takes a man to do this – "Well done, Michael."'

Where Mendy is right – and Benn would not disagree – is in identifying that fight as the turning point in his career. What happened afterwards probably made Benn as a top-line fighter, more so than any of his other big nights, because he not only returned to the fire, he went looking where it was hottest: America. Without Watson, I doubt there would have been a McClellan.

First up in his rehabilitation there was Jorge Amparo, who took him the full ten rounds in his stateside debut, in Atlantic City in October 1989. José Quinones didn't extend him in the one round it lasted when Benn went to Las Vegas for the first time, in December, but Sanderline Williams, a cagey customer, taught Benn a thing or two in losing to him over ten back on the boardwalk.

When Benn stepped up to challenge Doug De Witt for the WBO middleweight title in the same town in April, he survived a serious examination of his will and his chin, before stopping the American in the eighth. 'The Nigel Benn that beat Doug De Witt would have beaten any middleweight in the world,' says Manny Steward. 'And I mean any middleweight, then, now or any time.'

Then came perhaps the Londoner's most riotous performance of all. Mendy recounts how Benn got through his fight with 'The Blade', Iran Barkley, a fighter whose stare could crack pavements.

'To my mind,' Mendy recalled, 'Nigel had two great fights in his life, two great fights and he never had a bad fight. But the two great fights, one was against a guy called David Noel at Crystal Palace when he totally, totally changed everything. It was the most perfect, complete display of boxing you could wish to see, and the second was Iran Barkley.'

Terry Marsh had accompanied Mendy and Benn to Atlantic

City, along with another old friend, Vic Andreetti, who had taken over Nigel's training. They had a great time rabble-rousing around Miami but this was business. And Barkley, an erratic force, was still hugely dangerous. He won two more world titles after this one, including a win over Thomas Hearns at light-heavyweight. Nigel had reason to be concerned.

'We were in the changing room before the fight,' says Mendy, 'and I'd ask everyone to step outside the changing room, and then we'd hug and embrace . . . because you never knew what was going to happen. Nigel was my friend, and we'd come through all these things together, and there we were, two East End kids, out in America, it was the hottest ticket in town, and everybody you can care to mention, Tom Hanks, Tom Selleck, just happens to be sittin' ringside.'

Benn was shaking his head and hands manically, to the beat of his pre-fight music. Mendy told him to 'stop mucking about'. Benn shouted back, 'I'm not mucking about! Do you know this fella can do serious damage to me?'

The referee knew what both fighters were capable of, the way they fought. He told them beforehand to keep it reasonably clean and he'd just let them get on with it.

In centre ring, he said, 'You two guys want a war? You got a war. If you ain't bitin' or kickin', I ain't there. Defend yourselves at all times. Seconds out!'

Benn was totally focused. He was going to tuck up under Barkley's expected charge, duck and dive on the ropes, then launch hooks around his guard before covering up again. He hoped to confuse the American this way, then overpower him. It was a reasonable strategy. Then followed a delay of about thirty seconds, because the TV coverage had not come back on schedule. It was a timely respite.

Andreetti shouted up to Benn from the corner. 'Nigel!'

Benn could barely hear him.

'Nigel!' the trainer shouted again.

'Yeah?'

'You know all that stuff I been teachin' ya, the tactics and what-ever?'

'Yeah, yeah, I know, Vic! Leave me alone!'

'Well, fuck all that, Nige! Just knock this cunt out!'

And he did.

'Nigel ran forward,' Mendy recalls, 'faked to the left, faked to the right, faked to the left. Bang! And all of a sudden there was Barkley sittin' on the middle rope and Nigel tryin' to take his head off. What a great day that was. And I can't get away from the fact we're two black kids out of east London.'

That was then. But Mendy went and got caught robbing a bank and was back inside. Benn carried on fighting, and somewhere along the line they fell out.

'Nigel and me? No. Nigel and I don't speak . . .'

Mendy's view of their fallout is that it was a moral disagreement, an interesting position for a serial fraudster to take.

'When Nigel got married, I was his best man, we were in Las Vegas . . . We had a sit-down meeting, and I said to Nigel, "Nigel, there are things you do, and there are things you don't do," and, without going into it, I made it crystal clear that if these things continued to happen, I couldn't be there. Not only was I his friend, but he was now asking me to be the friend of his wife and his children. Our children are the same age, my younger children. I got two adults as well. But my younger children. We've got three whose ages coincide. But what I asked never stopped. What I asked Nigel to stop doin', he wouldn't do.

'He then found a clown who knew about as much about boxing – Peter DeFreitas – as I know about nuclear physics, and I've got a physics A Level, so I'm puttin' that in perspective. Ultimately, Nigel is the kinda guy, you put him in a room with himself and he's gonna fall out with himself. That's his nature.'

Benn didn't see it like that. Where Mendy objected to Nigel's extra-curricular activities, Benn saw Mendy's weakness for a scam as a liability. He'd admired him as a guru when out and about the clubs of London's West End but, as in most relationships in boxing, he grew away from him as he became more confident of his own standing in the business. Mendy could see he was gradually losing control of the young man who had once idolised him.

Benn had been attracted to Mendy's flashiness the first time they met. Here was a black man making it on his own, looking the part. There were girls and good times. Fast cars and excitement. Celebrities at every table in every club. Benn had money and he had the energy. Mendy was just the guy to help him enjoy himself, to give him the sharp allure of a proud and successful black hero. This was a black thing. Any of his white friends, such as Rolex Ray, could only be attendants to the court. Mendy aimed high. He really did see himself as the next Don King and to go for that there was just one place: only in America.

The States suited Benn, not to mention Ambrose and Rolex Ray and all the others. He was away from home, learning the boxing smarts in Miami from some wise old gym rats and, at night, he was partying strong. He could manage it, no problem. He was young and fit, 'up for it'.

Nigel himself admits he was playing hard at night. 'While in Miami, I met a dancer who was with an all-girl group. She was really sexy and the first time I made love to her I thought I was going to die. It was explosive!'

A lot of his life has been like that. He is honest enough, at least, to say his promiscuity has caused him and his women much personal grief. Sharron and the kids read all about his night with Lois when she sold her story of their bedroom gymnastics. Lois claimed Nigel licked strawberries and cream from her more intimate areas – which prompted the *Sun*'s Colin Hart (or, more likely, his sports-desk) to arrange for strawberries and cream to be delivered to Benn before the Amparo fight.

Where it all went wrong for Benn and Mendy is anyone's guess. Money probably had something to do with it; it always does. But, sifting through their conflicting versions, it is likely it was a power-personality clash. Both wanted to be the main man. Only Benn could lay claim to that, realistically. It was he who had been the champion, he was the one generating the money. Ambrose was there to entertain and facilitate. Where Ambrose had been the charismatic guru, now he was hired help. It was a mirror to what was to happen between McClellan and Steward.

For Benn and Mendy, the rift would simply widen beyond repair. Benn knew more about the business than Mendy did because he had been in it for longer. He saw fighters and managers split all the time. He'd split with a couple himself already, most notably Frank Warren. He'd seen Terry Marsh fall out with Warren, he'd seen his friend Colin McMillan return from New York once after trying to do a deal with Don King looking like some mobster had just put the frighteners on him. No, there wasn't much naivety left in Nigel when he came to have his rows with Ambrose. And he certainly was not taking any lessons in morality from a man who, according to his own version of events, had accompanied him to a Glasgow bordello and brought his son.

'Ambrose?' Benn says, ready for the obvious. 'Good salesman, done a good job, but he done a lot of things he shouldn't have done. That's the way he is. It's in him. If he can get away with it, he'll do it. He got away with a lot of things. It took me a long time to get used to all that in boxing, right up until the end of my career even.'

The man Benn did have respect for, Don King, was everyone's favourite villain.

'It's like the movie, *Only in America*, about Don King. "Here's a contract, don't worry, I'll fill it in later." That's me! I been in that situation with him. But I like Don King, I ain't got a bad word to say about Don King.'

Benn understands boxing's unique morality. He understands King.

'Let me tell you something: when Don King paid me a million pounds to fight Chris Eubank, I don't care if he made twenty million, I'm happy with what I got. And that's what a lot of people forget.' This sounded like the advice Stan Johnson gave McClellan.

Then Benn met Tyson. They got on almost straight away, even if Tyson often showed his animal side in public, Benn saw the rampaging heavyweight as 'powerful and intimidating'. In a Las Vegas nightclub he watched women coming up to the fighter for kisses and autographs. Every time they got close, Tyson asked if he could touch the girl's pussy, as Benn put it. 'He would grab every girl within reaching distance.'

DeFreitas, who moved into the management set-up about this time, eventually supplanting Mendy, remembers other aspects of their relationship. He especially remembers the end, Benn's last fight on 9 November 1996, in Manchester against Steve Collins. It was the night Naseem Hamed unleashed his intemperate blast at Benn for quitting in the sixth. Naz said he would have fought on, without arms and legs, all the usual over-the-top stuff that fighters say.

'Let me explain something to you,' says DeFreitas, in the way that sounded like it was a preface to a threat. 'I stopped it. Not many people know this, but Nigel should never have been in there in the first place. He had a shadow on the brain. Only myself and the British Boxing Board of Control knew. I felt it was my duty to approach his family, without Nigel knowing, and ask them what they felt. So I speak to his dad, and his brother John, who works for him. They said, provided he's monitored every fight, we haven't got a problem with it. If it deteriorates, I'd explained to them that the board would stop him fighting anyway. He was legal, though. Nigel kept saying to me, even before McClellan, "Why've I got to keep havin' these scans? It's supposed to be once a year, innit?" I said, "Nige, you're fighting world-title fights, don't worry 'bout it." So I got him round it.

'Then after the Collins fight we went to Harley Street, and a doctor told him he had a lesion. It hadn't got any worse. But it was there.'

Nevertheless, Benn seriously contemplated a comeback. He rang his old friend, Jimmy Tibbs. 'Come down and I'll see what you've got left,' Tibbs said.

Tibbs, who was in Watson's corner the night he was hurt against Eubank, did not know about Benn's neurological problem. The comeback, often written about in the tabloids, never happened. He wasn't to know it, but that decision would prove to be frustrating to another member of the McClellan family, a fighter who wanted to exact revenge on Nigel for what happened to Gerald. His brother Todd.

Gutteridge: '[Benn has] revived body and spirit, after what could have been a disastrous opening round.'

Watt: 'He has to keep coming forward. He can't allow McClellan to back him up. Benn has had no trouble getting the punches home, Reg. McClellan's defence is very sloppy.'

Reg makes the observation that this is the Benn of old, when he knocked them over early and complained his opponents were 'Mexican roadsweepers'. McClellan, points out Gutteridge, 'is a long way from that'.

But, as Watt says, 'McClellan still hasn't solved Benn's style. He's been missing with the straight, long right and he's not coming back with the left hook, so Benn is keeping out of trouble.'

And now the blinking starts in earnest again. Benn swipes a left hook across the front of McClellan's eyebrows and Gerald is confused rather than hurt. It is a punch no more damaging than the one thrown by Carl Sullivan in Atlantic City, the one that made Gerald's eyes 'sting a little'. Gerald is blinking hard. The mouthguard comes out again.

Benn lands one-off lefts and rights with nothing coming back.

Watt: 'I think Benn has shocked McClellan with his punching power and his heart. McClellan is hanging on here.'

Gutteridge: 'He's like a sailor clinging on to a mast, Jim. They're not baffling each other with science but the East Enders here are really lapping it up.'

It is obvious that Gerald's boxing is losing shape. He misses again with the right but, against all he'd been taught by Milwaukee Al, Stan, Manny and Willie Brown, he doesn't compensate then for the wayward right with a following left hook to cover the gap. Benn knows McClellan is weakening.

Watt: 'Reg, something has got to give.'

7

Rounds Five and Six   *Dog Meat*

Albert: 'McClellan switching to southpaw . . . A right hand by Benn!'

Pacheco: 'That switching is a waste of time, because what's happening to him is he is being outspeeded and out-thought.'

Albert: 'A thumping left hook by Benn! McClellan looks confused. The cagey Nigel Benn seems to have gained control of this fight. Benn's got a second wind. He's been resurrected after that near knockout in the first.'

Pacheco: 'Gerald's fighting with his mouthpiece hanging half out, he's getting tired . . .'

Albert: 'It usually means fatigue is setting in. McClellan apparently not throwing the right with real intentions. He had surgery on the right hand, after his last fight. He's been out nine and a half months. I wonder if that is factoring in now?'

Pacheco: 'He better forget about it for now, because he's got a tiger on top of him right now . . . He's about to lose his mouthpiece. He cannot breathe correctly. That mouthpiece gives him some . . .'

Albert: 'Ferocious exchange! Toe to toe in the centre of the ring! Fifteen seconds to go in the fifth. The mouthpiece continues to hang out . . .'

Pacheco: 'But he's doing a little bit better in the punching. He's outpunching Benn.'

They were both, in fact, missing.

Albert: 'So here at the London Arena, in London, England, we are between rounds five and six in a fight that has become a war.'

Everyone goes on about the dogs. Most people were shocked by the stories. Gerald, after all, was 'a nice kid'. What was it with the dogs?

In Las Vegas in 1994, when McClellan was preparing for his rematch with Jackson, the one-eyed hitter he'd stopped the year before to win his world middleweight title, he was in his hotel room. He was bored, anxious. He got a video out and slipped it in the machine. The fight was only a few hours away. It was the biggest of his career to that point. There was nobody about and the world champion settled down to get his kicks.

As the tape rolled, Stan Johnson knocked on the door.

'He's some guy,' Stan recalls. 'I think he'd be in his room before a fight, gettin' a little pussy or somethin' before he go to the fight ... well, Gerald be in the room this time watchin' tapes of dogfights. I thought he be watchin' a sex movie. But I goes into the fuckin' room, Gerald's got a tape of himself watching the dogs with a stockin' over his head where you can't see who he is – in case somebody find the tape no one know it's him!'

This is how Stan saw Gerald and the whole dog thing:

'So he got this black Labrador, just went to the dog shop, told the man, "I need a dog to take care of, I'll take this Labrador home," and the man say to the dog, "Yeah, you got a good home now," and Gerald takes the dog home. He takes the dog down his basement and tapes the Labrador's mouth, takes his pit bull Deuce and says "Get him!" He lets Deuce start eatin' the dog up while he's timing it on a watch, see how long it would take his dog to kill this dog. And I said to Gerald, "Hey, Gerald, the pit bull's a vicious dog and they learn to fight anyway, and this Labrador wouldn't beat Deuce, no way, so why did you tape his mouth shut?" And he said, "Coz I just wanna see how fast my dog would kill him, for one, and, for two, my dog's a championship fighter and you don't need no dog scratched up and bit up by no dog, by no accident. This is like sparrin' for my dog, this is like my dog need to taste blood every day. My dog need to kill somethin' every day, Stan. Just like a fighter need to spar every day, needs to work, he don't need nobody bustin' him up when he got a big fight comin' up. He just need to bust somethin' up hisself. Right?"'

Stan spoke with authority about dreadful events and it was impossible not to be mesmerised by the rhythm of the telling, and by the tale itself. It was almost musical and only partly translates into print. Brilliantly ungrammatical. It was a kind of rapping, old-style ghetto cool-speak, all mixed up like a cheap stew, bits of profanity chucked in to pepper it up. Comfort language served up by a badass dude.

Gerald got his comfort between the sheets. Any time of the day or night.

'It was nothin' for him to get some pussy just time afore he go in the ring, even, you know? So that was the main problem with Gerald, it was girls was his problem. But Gerald had a dark side to him, because he was a violent, violent, violent, violent, violent person.' I had to check: that was five 'violents'. Stan was just making sure.

'His whole life was about fightin' and all, pit bull dogs, he pay lotsa money on dogfights, he took money from his fights and he bet. It weren't nothin' him go down the projects in Chicago and bet $10,000 his dog beat your dog. And a bunch o' gang bangers with guns and drugs all come down to watch the fightin' and that . . .'

Donnie Penelton, the Black Battle Cat, he remembers the dogs. He was there too on those dark nights.

'Yeah, Gerald's my first cousin. We grew up together. I'm older than him, and from the age about three, four, he hangin' around buggin' me from about then, yeah. He was a nice, young scary kid. He was a maniac with the pit bull dogs, man. He was like one hisself. Very aggressive. Very crazy. He had like a yard full of pit bulls. We'd mostly take 'em to Detroit with us, to the camps. I didn't like watchin' them dogs fight like that, I guess . . . Kinda difficult, but them dogs, they goin' to fight naturally anyway. You know what he say, though? He always say, "Goddam, if I gotta fight for a livin', I be damned if them dogs ain't gotta fight for a livin' too. I gotta buy 'em their food. If it's a big fight and they win, they oughta be buyin' their own damn food."'

Donnie laughs.

'One of his favourite ones was called Deuce. . . . And I remember one time Gerald left another dog, his girl pit bull, with Willie Brown. Me and him went somewhere, coming back, and Willie Brown let the dog get out. We rode around all that night in Detroit . . . never did find that dog. Yeah, he cried before he couldn't find that dog.'

Deuce was the star of Gerald's Vegas hotel video. In interviews after a fight, he would often point to the Deuce tattoo on his right

McClellan shows a reporter a tattoo of his favourite pit bull, Deuce. After Deuce lost, Gerald wondered about the bloodthirsty side of his nature. © Vanessa Winship.

arm. He'd say hello to everyone in Freeport. His family. But always he'd remember Deuce.

'He loved that dog so much,' Stan said. 'He brought Deuce down to fight this guy's dog in Chicago one time, and me and Donnie, we went down there with him . . . Gerald was drivin' his Mercedes Benz, a green car with caramel-coloured seats and he had this big, beautiful truck behind where he carried his dogs in cages. So Deuce, he winnin' this particular dogfight and all of a sudden the dog got on him and he started rippin' Deuce's throat out. So I'm kinda, like, lookin' at Gerald coz I was always, like, kinda wonderin' what kinda guy this was, you hear what I'm sayin'? And I was lookin' at him and I was seein' the 'spressions on his face, you know, and just as his dog was gettin' beat, Gerald told the dude, "Stop the fight!" And the dude said, "No, man. No, man, you started the fight." And Gerald says, "You stop this motherfuckin' fight! Stop the fight! I quit, here your money."

'Gerald had a nice green leather suit on, he picked his bloody dog up, threw his dog across his shoulder, blood run all down his fuckin' coat. Instead o' puttin' him in the truck, in the cage, he put him in the back seat o' the Benz, mad as hell, rubbing his dog, cryin' up and down the road, tellin', "I ain't never gonna do this shit no more, I don't know why I did this, I keep a mess o' snakes afore I put a dog through this again." You know? . . .

'Yeah, Gerald he had some companionship about this particular dog. He'd raised this dog, and this dog, he'd killed a few. This fucking guy, man, once his dog lost a fight and he was $7,000 down. He turns around, he looks at me, and the other guy says, "Hey, you want to wash your dog off before you put him in your truck?" Gerald just pulls a nine-millimetre out of his back pocket, aims it at the dog's head, busts a cap to the dog's head, and says, "Put that motherfucker in a plastic bag. I don't need 'em if they can't fight no better than that. I don't need no motherfuckin' dog that can't fight." This the kinda guy he was . . .'

I knew before I started that some of this story wasn't going to make easy listening, but this kind of information was confusing. It was not just hard-core boxing stuff; it was the sound of streets I didn't really know. But Gerald and Stan felt at home there. So did

Tyson. Listen to Iron Mike's angrier outbursts: he is shouting at the largely white world and he is saying, I'm going home to the streets and you can't come. It's the place that Don King calls home. He's another big hitter comfortable with the argot.

Gerald wasn't a million miles from Don King in his attitude to humanity. King had brought grief – and money – to a lot of lives. He was cold too. Gerald hadn't killed anybody, as King had, but he had that streak in him, an icy vein of ruthlessness. He had to have it. He knew what was demanded to survive in the 'baahxin' bizness'. If you didn't have a hard outside, they'd eat away at your insides and spit you out. That's one thing he learnt from King.

Gerald was not shy of conflict. Used to go looking for it, often. It was part of his protective shell. Getting in the ring and throwing his well-schooled punches for three, regulated minutes per round was a run in the park for Gerald – after all he'd seen outside boxing. His personality was not informed by his trade, but by his life at large. The boxer is just the product. A celebrity. Television packages him and sells him. The G-Man. The Dark Destroyer. Iron Mike. The Hit Man. The Beast. Midnight. Vicious. The Black Battle Cat. Nightmare. All names invented to disguise the man underneath, not describe him.

I could only wonder what else they got up to. Stan, unsurprisingly, had a million stories.

'We in Florida one time,' says Johnson, 'we in trainin', just before we go to fight Nigel Benn. Gerald says, "You wanna go to the mall to do some shoppin'?" So we go to the mall with the champ to do some shoppin', and we come outta the mall, and in Florida you got these pretty little pelican birds, what you call 'em? Flamingos, that's it. They just walk around the mall tryin' to make it look pretty. But Gerald comes out, and he says, "Right, watch this, watch this!" And there's this flamingo kinda walkin' around on the road. Gerald gets close to the 'mingo and makes a dip with the car, he speeds the car up real bad and – boom! – he hits the damn flamingo! And the flamingo flies up all over the grille! And Gerald, he's laughin', like it's all in Disneyland, and he goes flyin' round the block and he looks at the grille and he looks at the bird feathers and he pulls the bird feathers and pulls the bird outta the grille, and, it's like, "Damn! Did you all see that? Did you all like that?" And then he was on his way out – and you know, you can go to jail for doin' that sort of shit, you know? That's a state bird! You know what I mean?'

I know what you mean, Stan.

'So then Gerald goes around again! He already run over a couple of pelicans and then here come another pelican and you know, like, this motherfuckin' pelican must be wonderin' what's goin' on here, like? He must be like a brother or sister, like, they all busted up. And then Gerald, he says, "Look at this nosy sonofabitch, watch this." And – bam! – he rammed over that one. I said, "Gerry, you gotta stop this, man, we gonna go to jail." And he tried to make it look like it's an accident, that the bird was there, like . . . The kid was a violent kid. He loved killin' shit, he loved dog fights, like it was evident, he was want to go out like he went out . . .'

Like Deuce. Except he made Deuce quit.

As they go back for the sixth, Hamed is convinced Benn has it won. 'Great fight for Nigel. I can see him takin' him out. Two more rounds. Nigel's looking the stronger fighter. He's taken the punishment, he's coming back with the punches. Believe me, it's Nigel's night. Once I got into the place tonight, I knew there'd be an upset.'

The commentators, not having the benefit of Naseem's prescience, are left to go on what they see in front of them. And, as Showtime and ITV see it, it's not looking pretty for Gerald in the sixth.

Albert: 'McClellan seems to be having trouble now breathing through his big mouthpiece . . .'

Pacheco: 'A butt there on the part of Gerald, nothing happened . . . but it was a good butt.'

Albert: 'Gerald holds him with one hand, Nigel hits him with the other.'

Pacheco: 'The referee's much too fussy for my taste, much too fussy . . . Gerald's got to do something to turn this around. These rounds are beginnin' to pile up on him. He's doing something he never did before: punch once or twice and watch. He would always throw three or four punches. But he's not doing that now.'

Benn ties McClellan up, bangs him about the back of the head. Gerald complains.

Pacheco: 'That's bad news. He shouldn't even bother with the referee. He's got a guy in front of him.'

And water underneath. He slips near Benn's corner. Looks down at the floor. Distracted. Unfocused. Troubled. Rather be somewhere else. At a dog-fight maybe. Getting a little pussy somewhere maybe. Back home. Back in Freeport. Anywhere but London, England.

Benn is the physically wearier of the two, but mentally stronger. He leans on McClellan in a corner, belting his body listlessly, just enough to take away Gerald's boxing. McClellan punches his way clear, but takes a left hook as he moves off. McClellan's coasting, gloves dropping. Benn shoots over a right that pops Gerald's mouthpiece out of his mouth.

Albert: 'Whoa! There goes the mouthpiece! It was hanging precariously the last few rounds. They're still going at it . . . after the bell!'

Benn is back on the street now. Belting McClellan around the neck, up the side of his head. Mugging done, he sneers, walks to his corner, stops, hands on hips, gestures after Gerald. He's won this right here.

Watt: 'For sheer excitement, Reg, this one rates with any of the fights I've ever seen, in all my years in the fight game.'

McClellan looks spent, spitting clear some phlegm as he slumps on to his stool. Stan takes the mouthpiece from the referee and turns to attend to his fighter . . . Benn's round. At the Showtime mike, there is the first sign of concern that something is not right.

Pacheco: 'Boy, this thing's taking a nasty turn for Gerald McClellan . . .'

8

Round Six and a Half *'Sometimes, Nothin' is a Real Cool Hand . . .'*

The art of deception practised by fighters is as natural to them as breathing.

To make your opponent believe that you are his superior, you have to first convince yourself of the fact. If you think it is so, there is usually no problem. You will then have the confidence to express that perceived superiority without the fear of penalty. Any deficiencies will be disguised by the power of your performance, and the reluctance of your opponent to challenge you.

However, if you already believe – or are constantly told – that your opponent is stronger, smarter, more committed, or if you discover this unpalatable truth early in the fight, you have to lie to yourself, and then to your opponent. You have to pretend you are better than you are. If you do not, you are doomed.

In the light of this reality, if your ambition is still to win, you have to disguise your lie. A double deception. Even if you want only to survive, to reach the final bell relatively undamaged, you must still tell half-truths. You have to absorb pain while giving the impression it is not going to make you quit. If your opponent (who is almost certainly playing the same game) suspects you are kidding him, that your spirit is weak and you would accept defeat if it were imposed heavily on you, his confidence and his strength will grow. If his original aim was to win, he will now try to impose his will on you.

Boxing always was the lying game.

When Gerald returned to his corner at the end of the sixth round, he was through with lying. He had known since the second round that something was not right. He was labouring for breath; his right hand, which he'd hurt in banging out Julian Jackson, throbbed. There was, he would say a short time afterwards in the few coherent moments left to him, 'water rushing in my head'. And he was blinking, blinking, blinking. Like a man with a nervous tic.

'I wanna quit, Stan.'

Lisa says she has the words on tape. She gave the tape to an FBI investigator who was on Don King's case for a variety of alleged, ultimately unproven, crimes. Frank Warren told me in the week after the fight that he'd heard a rumour that Gerald said he'd had enough after six rounds. Brendan Ingle, who was in the corner but down below the stool on which McClellan sat, says he couldn't hear clearly what was being said.

Johnson at first told me he didn't remember Gerald saying he wanted to quit. Then he said, flatly, it didn't happen. These are words he says Gerald would never say. In fact, Gerald had said to him before the fight that he would kill Stan if he pulled him out. Donnie confirms this. And they both say Gerald meant what he said.

Lisa acknowledges that Gerald might well have 'threatened' Stan and Donnie before the fight. She also says her brother was wrong to have them there in the first place. The last people Gerald needed in his corner were two guys afraid to disagree with him. The man he needed was Manny Steward. That's the way Lisa sees it.

Lisa, going on the tape she sent to the FBI, says Stan sounded like he was in charge. 'Gerald said at the end of the sixth round that he wanted to quit and Stan said, "You get your ass back out there, you fight, and you gonna fight until you die, you gonna fight, you gonna finish this fight if it kills you."'

Her loathing for Stan is intense. 'Like, with Stan, all Stan cared about was gettin' paid. But Donnie told me that he wanted to stay in London with Gerald, and Don King told them to go home. Don got the three of them together and told them. He paid them, whatever . . . whatever Gerald agreed . . . I think he gave Stan, like, $10,000. And he told 'em to go back to Milwaukee to keep their motherfuckin' mouths shut and don't discuss nothin'.'

Johnson admits he had strong words with Gerald, roughly along the lines of Lisa's account, but that this was regulation boxingspeak. He is more puzzled as to how she knew, because neither the British nor American tapes of the between-round conversation pick up on the exchange. He and Donnie also agree that King did not want them around after the fight, and they left almost straight away. But then King was a bigger control freak than Gerald was. Where Stan and Lisa agree is their suspicion that King wanted everyone to go home so he could get hold of the fight contract in case there were any arguments about the figures later. It's just that Lisa reckons Stan was in on that deal; Stan resolutely says he was not. King, meanwhile, refused to speak to me about the fight, despite several requests – a rare instance of Don clamming up.

But that was history. McClellan could only play the cards he was dealt. It is clear there was confusion in the corner. I was maybe fifteen feet away and could see a lot of arm-waving and anxious faces. It should have been over by now. Gerald said so. Stan and Donnie too. But instead their champion was sitting in front of them, tired and confused. Blinking, blinking, blinking. He now had to confront the unpalatable: the prospect of defeat. Forget Milton and Ward. This was real defeat coming up, the sort Heenan dealt with by trying to strangle Sayers – or Tyson's way, the night he took a chunk out of Holyfield's ear. The exits were rushing at him on a highway to nowhere.

Ingle was the only impartial witness to what happened in Gerald's corner at the end of the sixth round. The Sheffield trainer had secured himself one of the best seats in the house that night, 'handing up', as it's called. He liked this extra duty at big fights. Better than sitting in the cheap seats. Good craic. Ernie Draper, who works in an all-embracing capacity for Warren, had paid Brendan £20 to hold Gerald's spit bucket and pass up the accoutrements of the fighter's kitbag.

Ingle, who had seen his share of backstage confusion during the final few fights in which he trained Naseem Hamed, was astounded at the performance of Gerald's seconds. 'It was a strange set-up in the corner. There was no harmony. You could feel the tension.'

Stan and Donnie don't admit to any friction but Brendan says he heard that Gerald had had a fight with Stan beforehand. Nobody else remembers it. But Brendan maintains, 'He hits the fellow and knocks his teeth out. He [Stan] was a complete idiot. I thought to myself, "What are you doing in the bloody corner with him?" Anyway, I'm listening to this fella, he's just shoutin' and bawlin'. You couldn't understand what he was sayin'. There was no constructive dialogue in the corner at all. I think McClellan made a terrible mistake sacking his trainer and getting this fella in, the fella with the sailor's cap.

'I thought Gerald looked pretty distressed. His mouthpiece was sticking out. What happened to him was he got sick of hitting Benn in the early rounds. And that's a fact. It just completely done his head in. Because when he come back to the corner at the end of the first round, he was shaking his head, and he said, "I've hit him with everything." None of us could quite believe that Benn was still standing.'

Now, in that crucial halfway fog, between rounds six and seven, McClellan needed someone he could trust, to interpret his scrambled thoughts and advise how best to overcome his crisis. This was not a time or place for indecision. If McClellan was incapable of working through his dilemma himself, of conquering his own doubts, Stan and Donnie were his only refuge.

Ingle saw another angle to the row he claims Gerald had with Stan before the fight. 'You can't have favourites in the gym,' he says. 'You must treat everyone the same. You've got to be seen to be fair. And the other problem is the kids have got to listen to you.' He struggles to articulate what is a crucial point. 'Either you've got to go, or they've got to go. Listen, someone's done something on you . . . you're better off walking away. You're in the position otherwise of getting them seriously hurt. Do you hear what I'm sayin' to you? You should be pullin' them out or you should be tellin' them somethin'. You've got to be their best friend. Sometimes that's not appreciated. Do you hear what I'm sayin' to you?'

Did Gerald have a friend in Stan or Donnie? They would contend that he did. Donnie'd known Gerald since he was four years old; Stan met Gerald when he was barely a teenager. They'd been tomcatting and gambling and dogfighting together. Christ, they'd killed flamingos together – and that's a fuckin' state bird!

But it wasn't that simple. In his entire boxing career, from the age of twelve through to the final fight fifteen years later, Gerald was never afforded the sanctuary of being regarded as a bum. He was always a star, and that carries its special pressures. McClellan, in short, was too good to quit. Winners don't have that option normally, because they are carrying the show not just for themselves, but for the promoters and managers around them. They also have their pride – and a lot of boxers have their pride chipped away at as their careers start to fade. They take the money and, with as much dignity as they can muster, they quit.

When Broughton sang out to the Duke of Cumberland, 'I'm blind but I'm not beat', he might have been subconsciously asking his patron to rescue him, to save his pride. Cumberland, the Don King of his day, turned and walked, leaving his champion to the booing of the crowd. In more civilised times, fighters send out signals of surrender in different ways. A bad cut can be a saviour. A broken hand claimed. Or, after being felled by a solid blow, a beaten boxer can hug the floor like a mother's apron, hoping the referee will see enough distress in his eyes to grant him mercy.

As a feared and distinguished champion, not to mention a moneymaker of significant reputation, McClellan had none of those options. He knew beforehand he was expected to be in this fight until there was nothing left to give. Stan and Donnie knew that too. Besides, they were being paid meagre wages and across the ring from them sat King, who would be distinctly upset if they pulled McClellan out of the fight. Those were the pressures, real or perceived, bearing down on the occupants of that corner at the end of round six.

As Ingle points out, you cannot afford to have acrimony in a boxer's corner. It can be a place of awful devilment. And paranoia. Before his two fights with Sonny Liston, Muhammad Ali was convinced the Mob would try to fix his water, and he went to great lengths to ensure what he drank between rounds was pure H_2O. That did not stop his black Muslim sponsors claiming that Ali's trainer Angelo Dundee (whose brother Chris knew nearly every gangster worth the name) had wiped some kind of blinding chemical on Ali's gloves in the first fight with Liston. Dundee, naturally, denies the allegation. When Sonny quit at the end of the sixth, the conspiracy theorists switched their gaze to the other corner. To this day, nobody is sure.

So, what was going on in Gerald's corner? Not much of a constructive nature, it seemed.

According to Sean Curtin, who oversees boxing for the state of Illinois, where Johnson often works, 'Stan's been around the block.' Stan, like Gerald, didn't reach the sixth round too many times in his own career, but for different reasons. In his later years as a serial loser, he didn't provide a contest so much as a body to hit. Donnie performed a similar function. They were not paid to win. Which is why, when Gerald, a born winner, told them not to argue with him, they didn't – they were not in a position to do so. They were employees, not figures of authority.

Let us assume that Gerald was in a bad way when he went to his stool for that precious minute's rest. Sixty seconds. That's not a long time for an in-depth discussion about a person's immediate future on the planet. You take out the mouthpiece (which had been hanging out precariously since late in the second round), wash it, wipe down Gerald's face to clear sweat from around his eyes, apply vaseline to bruised extremities, attend to any nicks or cuts with adrenalin, cool down his arms and chest, give him room to stretch his legs, to let his engine idle before revving it up again. These are tasks that have to be conducted with automatic ease, and Stan performed his duties competently.

Where he might have fallen down, according to Ingle, is in talking to his fighter. If McClellan's brain was starting to shut down, no amount of shouting or exhortation will have made much difference. Words will have formed an oral blanket around him as he tried to gather together his inner strength, but they will not have penetrated. The time for tactical talks had passed. McClellan had to fall back on instincts now, because fatigue had taken a terrible grip on him. In fact, it had been with him since the end of the first round. According to Donnie, Gerald was 'breathin' heavy, breathin' heavy'.

Under sustained pressure from Benn, all McClellan's admirable skills deteriorated noticeably after round two. His jab was missing, he moved into rather than away from Benn's overhand right, the McClellan left to the ribs was not functioning well. In short, his weapons had seized up. They surfaced later, when he got a second wind, but, after he was hurt early, his boxing gradually came apart. That is when an authoritative corner should have moved. That is the point, say around the fourth round, where a quick, decisive instruction should have been issued. Donnie recalls that, at the end of the second round, he implored Gerald to keep his hands up, to avoid Benn's overhand right. He did so only intermittently, getting hit often enough to become increasingly confused.

There were two early punches that appeared to put Gerald's boxing out of kilter. The first came towards the end of the first round, after he'd had Benn in trouble. It was a desperation hook that caught McClellan just behind the right ear. Instantly, his legs and arms lost their zip. Then, in the second, he was similarly stopped in his tracks – although even several replays of the tape will not identify the blow definitely. It's likely it was not just a single shot that did the damage, but several. But his corner should have noticed something, either then or at the end of the round. And, from rounds two to seven, they certainly must have been aware of the build-up of damage.

The question therefore lingers: given that there was obviously a problem, who should have stepped in to save Gerald from himself? Monsieur Asaro, the referee, disclaims responsibility. 'If you want to look for responsibilities, you have to look in the American's corner, where his men perhaps failed to do their job,' Asaro told Radio Monte Carlo two days after the fight. 'If I had felt that either boxer was in trouble I would have stopped the match. None of them complained to me about anything.'

This is simply not true. McClellan complained several times to the referee that Benn was hitting him at the back of the head. In fact, oddly, the referee admitted at the time, '[McClellan] had difficulties breathing and he couldn't hold his gumshield. He told them he had headaches.'

Presumably, on his own evidence, he did not know this first-hand. Otherwise, he would surely have had to intervene. And, anyway, he was rarely more than a few feet away from Gerald. He surely must have seen what the rest of us could clearly see. Gerald was having trouble breathing.

But he told Radio Monte Carlo, 'It was a violent fight but it was close and nothing allowed me to stop it. Until the tenth round McClellan never gave the impression that he was in trouble. He was leading for two judges and the third had it a draw. When a boxer is tired and says so, his cornermen can react. They can ask one of the three doctors to take a look at their boxer during the minute's rest. Only the referee can stop the bout but the minute's rest belongs to the cornermen.'

Asaro still works the rings of Europe. I saw him officiate in a fight on Eurosport in 2000 and he had lost none of his sense of laissez-faire. Alfred likes to let a fight run its course. His style of refereeing suits the physical fighter who wears down an opponent, and many of the old school would argue this is what boxing's about.

If a referee were merely an interpreter of rules, someone who penalises and watches, keeping the boxers in line, you might say that Asaro was a good referee. If, however, you believe a referee has more responsibility than that and should be pro-active in saving a brave boxer from himself, M. Asaro is a poor referee. Either way, the Parisian with hardly a word of English and a reluctance to stop a fight no matter what the carnage unfolding in front of him was the worst possible choice to be officiating in a bout between Benn and McClellan. Two dangerous men whose only second language was violence.

I rang Asaro at his Paris flat but, unarmed with French, had to ask him questions through a third party. This is his unedited defence.

'In boxing, the language is basically signs and English words. You don't speak to the boxers directly. It's an international language. You don't have the right to talk to them. Just four expressions: "Time", "Stop fighting", "Box", "Break". It's international, not French or English. Just those words.'

Did they understand you, though?

'The boxers understand you, because it's all gestures. When there is a reason to caution either boxer, you stop the action and you address the boxer concerned. Just by looking at him and, with gestures, you make sure that he understands you. By nodding your head, for instance, without saying anything, you are indicating that the fighter has been illegally hitting the head from behind, or you show him, perhaps, that he has been hitting below the waist. By pointing to the area concerned, you indicate that he should not be hitting the other fighter there. It's all gestures.'

Should Gerald's trainers have pulled him out of the fight before the end?

'The fight was a really hard one. All the press agreed I was not at fault. Personally, as a referee, I didn't realise that McClellan was suffering. There wasn't any time during the fight when McClellan was knocked flat on the floor. And, when he was KO'd, he just put one knee on the floor. Then I counted to ten. The only question is why the trainer never realised that McClellan was suffering so much. He would have been the only one who could have known. And you should bear in mind that, when the fight was stopped, McClellan was winning. I reckon he was leading by a couple of points. So nobody really noticed anything was wrong.'

But what about his mouthguard hanging out, from as early as the second round?

'As for his mouthguard hanging out, McClellan never spat it out on to the floor. He pushed it out, then back again, to breathe more easily, but it never fell out completely. So I had no right to stop the boxing for that reason alone. All boxers have the right to let their mouthguard hang out like that to breathe. If it comes out, though, and falls on the floor, obviously you stop the fight and have the boxer put the guard back again. And I insist that, if he had problems breathing, when he returned to his corner it was only his trainer who could have done something about it. It was up to the trainer. If he had done his job properly, he would have told me to bring the doctor to the corner to look at his fighter.

'I read English better than I speak it, but I hope you understand that in that fight nobody could have guessed what was going to happen. Perhaps the question you have to ask is did the fighter take some medication before the fight, because nobody understands why he collapsed the way he did.'

Where Asaro is at fault is in clinging to the slim defence that it was not his job to intervene. He is not just a referee but a guardian. He should have no consideration but interpreting the rules and watching for signs of extreme distress in either fighter. He is the ultimate authority. And, on that night, Alfred Asaro chose to stick to the book, as he understood his job. If he'd gone to McClellan's corner at the end of the sixth round, he might have heard an interesting conversation – except, of course, he doesn't speak English.

One of the best of all movie fights, inasmuch as it tore down the notion that strength is everything, was the one-sided affair between George Kennedy's jail bully and Paul Newman's rebellious loser in *Cool Hand Luke*. Newman (Luke) just keeps getting up. And Kennedy, a physical winner but mentally mugged, walks away confused. He could hit his man no more – just as McClellan got sick of hitting Benn for no obvious result. Luke staggers around the circling inmates. A beaten-up but unbeatable man, who'd come to the fight with no tools, a rank outsider.

Later, Luke wins a poker game with a truly garbage hand and Kennedy observes unwittingly the truth of their fisticuffs in the prison yard. He looks at Luke's cards and says, 'He won with nothin'! He didn't have nothin'!' To which Luke had but one reply, 'Sometimes nothin' is a real cool hand.'

It is. If you're a convincing liar. As all good boxers are.

At the end of the sixth, Gerald had nothing. Somehow, he conjured up a bit of artillery to go into four more terms, and would even look like winning it in the eighth. Benn knew McClellan was lying though. And he knew that the American had confronted that reality a few rounds before. At the end of six deals, McClellan was a busted flush. And, one way or another, he was trying to tell someone.

Except nobody listened.

McClellan played hard but didn't shirk his obligations in the gym. He'd been sweating hard since his father Emmite had him sparring under the street lights at the age of eight. © Vanessa Winship.

9

Lonely

'What say, Deuce? We in a corner here, boy. We in one bad place now, my friend. Sorry, Deuce, 'bout your fight. But that's what you born to do, that's what a fightin' dog does. And you were good until you met that motherfuckin' bitch that chewed you up. You know I loved you. That's why you had to go. What good a fightin' dog, Deuce, who can't fight no more? It ain't cruel you had to go. Just the way it is. Same for me, Deuce.

'Now I'm down to it, boy. I'm down to the damn bones, dog. This mother-fucker in the other corner, he's done some number on my head. Don't know what. Don't know what's goin' on. I'm throwin' 'em and he's not goin' down. They all go down when the G-Man throw 'em, Deuce! They all go down! 'Cept this motherfucker got up. How long ago was that? Three rounds s'all I need for most of 'em. Jackson . . . he was a mean hittin' man, he was up for the fight too, and he went over. The Beast, well, he weren't no beast no more when I met him, but you can't tell with the old guys, 'specially the good old guys. African too. Hard. Mugabi as hard as any of 'em. But the old Beast went down, Deuce. Three damn times he went down in one damn round, right here in London, England. Bang, good night, Beast, and the G-Man back in Freeport with his little world title quick as that.

'But this here's a proper belt, Deuce. This is big. This get me on the way to Jones, this motherfuckin' WBC belt. This title set the G-Man up for good. I'll chase down that Jones boy, and we'll get it on and everyone in the whole damn world'll know Gerald McClellan's the best fighter there is. Why, Deuce, I reckon I could knock out Mike Tyson. I do. When I·hit, they shit. They all do, don't they?

'Don't they, Deuce? . . . So why ain't this motherfuckin' Dark Destroyer goin' south yet? He's a hard one, all right. But his chin like any other. I gotta get my rhythm back. There's somethin' not right here, though. I know it. Don't feel right. My head's swimmin'. Can't breathe right. Gotta suck at the air real hard, Deuce. It's like I'm drownin'. Did I get hit? Yeah, I got hit. Few rounds ago, now.

'Where we now? That round six, just gone? Hell, I felt like quittin' then, Deuce. I did. Ain't never felt like that before. So there must be somethin' wrong. What in hell can it be? He didn't put me down, did he? Did he? Did he? Did he put me down? Where my legs gone, Deuce? Gotta get up now. Gotta go out again. Told Stan I'd kill him he try to stop this motherfuckin' fight. But why I bother to say that, Deuce? That never even entered my damn head before, in all my life. Never even thought that against Jones. Nobody ever gonna get on top o' the G-Man. So what in hell was I worried about?

'Gotta pin this motherfucker. Gotta get him good. This should be my fight. He's no slick boxer, not like those guys took me the distance. Milton, that his name? Yeah. And Ward? They just slick. Benn, he no fancy Dan boxer, just that crazy Brit, hookin' and duckin'. Any time I want I can box his smartass ears off. 'Cept he's everywhere. Can't line him up like I want to. But hell, I outboxed Roy fuckin' Jones fuckin' Jr!

'This worryin' me some, Deuce. Shouldn't have no worries. I'm the best. Why I worryin' even before the fight? What am I doin' givin' Stan and Donnie all those talks about "Don't you stop the motherfuckin' fight, else I kill ya"? You know, though, this one weird trip. Seems everything in my life got complicated. That Willie Brown, he's Manny's guy, he just upped and left. Stan and Donnie still there for me, and Junior, but it ain't all smooth for me. Story my motherfuckin' life. And that gym they put me in, the Peacock, whatever it called. There's that statue standin' outside of the front door, the one of Bradley Stone, man. Musta been a brave little guy. Died after his fight. Last year. But every damn day, Deuce, I gotta walk past that motherfuckin' statue they got of him, every damn motherfuckin' day. That be enough to do your fool head in. Anybody get to thinkin' 'bout dyin' walk past that statue every day. So I told Stan, I be like Bradley Stone, a warrior. That's what I am, Deuce. That's what you were too. But you got done, dog. I ain't gettin' beat here tonight by no Dark Destroyer. You made me strong, Deuce. 'Cept I can't find it, I got a gear or two missin'.

'What's happenin' to my head? This is bad, dog. Bad. They gettin' ready to push me off my stool now. Rest is over. Sendin' me out again, Stan and Donnie. Gotta find somethin'. Left to the liver, under the elbow, right cross, left hook. All I gotta do is put those on him. Then it be over. Gotta get a solution. Got to, Deuce. Otherwise, dog, you be seein' the G-Man sooner than you think.'

10

Rounds Seven and Eight   *'Be Not Afeard . . .'*

'Be not afeard: the isle is full of noises, sounds and sweet airs, that give delight, and hurt not.' – The Tempest, *Act 3, scene 2*

Nigel and Gerald were in their own tempest now. There was little about the tumult enveloping the London Arena that resembled comfort, either. It was a threatening, pervasive rumble of hate that had gathered at the ring, spewed towards them with a vulgar intensity by voyeurs whose awful mien was made worse by their very ordinariness. Decent people shouted for blood. They had been doing so since round one, fully twenty minutes ago. They would not spend that much time thinking about Third World Debt in a year. But here, in this steaming pit, they coalesced like a pack of wolves on the edge of a forest clearing, waiting for their champion to tear the invader limb from limb.

Albert: *'They can't even hear the bell. McClellan's still sitting . . . It is so loud in here!'*
   Pacheco: *'Well, McClellan doesn't look like he's interested to come out and do battle. He looks like he's losing heart.'*

At any fight, the baying of the mob fits the rhythm of the violence. As one man wilts, the drooling and snarling of the two-legged dogs seated out in the dark will hit a high. It is an involuntary and wholly uncharitable moving of the spirit.

   Tonight the ugly symphony was in good voice. Fuelled by the worst narcotics of spite, they wanted the American to suffer, to be hurt badly. If he had not been so good, if he had not been so arrogant, maybe it would have been different. But they saw him as a beast to be tamed. And Benn was their champion. He would do for them what they could not do themselves and, with every heavy blow, they would add their screams to the cause. This was what tribes at war must have sounded like.

What was fascinating about this fight, though, was how everyone lost the last vestiges of composure. The crowd, the cornermen, the commentators and, in the thick of it, the fighters. This was an animalistic representation of all the demons we keep hidden. It was out of control.

It had started between the sixth and seventh rounds, when Stan and Donnie urged Gerald to 'go out there and die'. It was not a reasoned discussion, but a battle cry. Johnson said later he had indeed used that language, but did not mean it in the literal sense. Lisa says the trainer was sending Gerald over the top, that he was shouting him into oblivion.

There was certainly a hail of words, a flailing of hands. All the time, Gerald sat emotionless and spent. When he got up to fight, it was with a practised skip. He might have heard half of what was said, but he was living in his own world now. There was no point in shouting at a man whose brain was flooded with confusion of another kind, internal dissent and doubt. As McClellan and Benn set their feet on the canvas for the seventh time of asking, the only conversation either was interested in was that short one between glove and jaw.

As his compatriots saw it, McClellan looked a reluctant, shell-shocked soldier. They wanted their champion, their representative of nationhood in the ring, to carry the fight for them. Pacheco, particularly, had turned into a cheerleader.

'Once again,' he says to Albert, 'McClellan waits and waits and waits. Stupid on his part. His corner's going to have to holler at him. He waits and the other guy throws.'

Albert reckons that Gerald 'looks like he's almost fighting in slow motion'.

Pacheco invokes the last card of the partisan observer: 'Benn just continues to score points with the judges. The judges are from Monterey, Bangkok and Switzerland.'

They're all looking for evidence of prejudice now. Where the judges are from might count if it goes to the wire.

Jim Watt, meanwhile, has spotted something above the din that has enveloped us all. 'This referee could ruin a good fight, Reg. He wants to get out of there. He's decided that's a low punch. He's given Benn some time to recover.'

Asaro had intervened. But Benn wanted no respite. He was flying. He desperately wanted to maintain the intensity of the fight. The crowd had lifted him to impossible heights and he was determined to stay there.

The seventh round is fairly even. McClellan has success in the middle stages but as the cacophony rises again, Benn revives near the bell. He thumps McClellan hard and often around the head, like he's tenderising steak. Gerald wilts, gets smaller, covers up, goes to the ropes, hangs on.

Pacheco notes, 'No damage done, but it looked good . . . for Benn.' Some truths are self-evident.

Watt and Gutteridge are keeping fairly cool heads. Reg, who's seen more fights than Joe Palooka, points out, 'It really is "anything you can do, I can do better" for Benn. He's got himself into great shape. That gumshield comes out again, Jim. I don't know. Maybe his nose is busted.'

Watt, a former world champion who knows what it's like to have your nose spread across your face, doesn't think so. 'I just think it's been the pace of the action. There's a craving for more oxygen and he's just got to open his mouth. McClellan's still trying to get a bit more composure into his work ... That was a tremendous left hook from Benn! That one really shook McClellan!'

Benn returned to his corner exhausted but exhilarated. He took a quick look around the Arena and saw the comforting wall of home insanity. This was his town, where football hooliganism held sway, where street hardness was identified by the colours of scarves rather than skin. He had his army with him, and they had shouted themselves into a hoarse frenzy, the likes of which few of us had witnessed.

A fighter needs encouragement. He is the most fragile of athletes, as well as often the most fearsome. The two qualities are not mutually exclusive, especially in Nigel Benn. Knowing Benn was to hook on to a rollercoaster, and in DeFreitas he had a manager every bit as manic and 'street' as himself.

DeFreitas knew Benn needed no more incentive than personal pride to get through this ordeal. He was a hugely proud man, humiliated once already in his career when he lost to Watson. That was not good. Nigel took some time – and distance – to get over that loss. Fully rehabilitated now after six defences of his world title, he felt confident and strong again. But, as ever with Benn, there were complications.

'He said to me, "Pete, I need to win this fight. Otherwise I'm skint."' That was the other incentive that kicked in now as Benn gathered his thoughts between rounds seven and eight. He was undeniably not coasting dosh-wise. He'd spent well, and he would earn good money again. But this was a crucial engagement for his banker.

DeFreitas had done the talking with King, who claimed he'd get him £6 million to fight Roy Jones. 'Between you and me,' DeFreitas confided later, 'Nigel wouldn't have a hope in hell against Jones. But I said to Nigel, "He can have the belt for fuckin' £6 million. Give it to him. Business is business, Nige."'

None of which concerns Benn as he prepares for the eighth round. The rounds are blurring now. The fight has stalled but could explode in an instant. The engagements are fitful. Neither fighter is sure of dominance. They have settled on an agreement, Benn and McClellan, that this is a hitter's fight. Load up, throw 'em – and see who's left standing. It is a decision they came to in the first thirty seconds. Nothing has dissuaded either man to change tack. The fight will rumble to a conclusion that is almost predetermined. The pact is signed. In the eighth round, however, there is another explosion.

For those of us still trying to remain detached, the eighth round was a big one for McClellan. For Dennie Mancini, it was a return to the nightmare of the second. 'At his best,' Mancini would say later, 'Nigel never had a great chin.'

And McClellan had a great punch. Bad combination for Benn. But then you never knew with Benn. We all remembered Logan; but we also remembered Watson. And the first Eubank fight. Would Benn fold now, after a brave effort? This is what I had thought beforehand, except I reckoned we would have got to this point about round five.

The reality, though, was that McClellan had been busted up. He had been physically and mentally wrecked by Benn's doggedness. McClellan never expected him to be there after three rounds, let alone eight. 'Three rounds is all anyone need,' he used to say. In effect, he had to fight two fights: the first, a disappointing engagement in which Benn refused to fold; the second, a war in which McClellan flirted with exhaustion, in which he shipped more punishment than he dealt out. But now, in that second fight, he looked like prevailing, finally. He had Benn in serious trouble. Surely he would finish him off this time. He had to. He had let him off in the first round, and suffered as a consequence. If he did not finish him now, would Benn come back at him again?

As McClellan clattered Benn's bruised head, the champion tried to calculate how long he had to suffer until the bell offered him a minute's rest. The American was making that calculation also, which informed his desperate attack. His punching was filled with as much venom as he had in him. There was no holding back, whatever his tiredness. He had to get the job done now or he risked letting Benn back into the fight in the next round.

Dennie always used to tell his fighters that the way to win a fight is to 'stay in there'. He had been around long enough to see fights go one way, then another. Not all the time, of course. But he'd seen Nigel fight plenty of times. He knew he could come back. He knew, if he really wanted it, he could overcome. And there had never been a moment's doubt, from the time Benn had signed for the fight, that he had wanted it. He knew they'd brought McClellan over to 'bash me up'. It was like being back on the street, and that was where Nigel Benn always felt comfortable.

Watt: 'Benn's people look the happier of the two parties. I think McClellan and his people must have thought they'd be sipping champagne already. They cannot believe that Nigel Benn is still here. Obviously, they were a bit complacent.'

No one mentioned anything about complacency to either of the two men in the ring.

Benn gunslings a left hook, catches Gerald, then ships another huge right himself. Back into a corner again for more trench warfare. Nigel looks gone. McClellan half-lands a finisher.

Albert: 'Right hand by McClellan!'

Gutteridge: 'Oh, he's done him! He rolls back from that punch, but he was hurt, Benn.'

Watt: 'The legs have dipped, Reg.'

Gutteridge: 'He's got to get out of that corner!'

Pacheco: 'And the referee's close to stoppin' this.'

Albert: 'Benn buckled over! A right hand by McClellan! Less than thirty seconds in the round! Down goes Benn!'

Pacheco: 'Benn is in horrible shape . . . Too much time to go. Too much time to go.'

Benn swings wildly and falls over. Asaro applies a standing eight count. Twenty-five seconds left.

Pacheco: 'Here comes McClellan! Here comes the Charge of the Light Brigade!'

Not quite.

Watt: 'Benn comes back with that left hook . . . Right hand from Benn!'

From somewhere, Benn finds an uppercut. They go at it close in. Gerald should be standing off but Nigel kids him into a clinch. Ties up those dangerous, dangerous arms. Digs a rib shot, a hook, a short right.

Gutteridge: 'We kept promoting this fight as explosive, Jim. But, I tell you what, we didn't promote it enough.'

Albert: 'What a round!'

What a round, indeed.

Mancini, resplendent in black satin jacket, yells at Nigel in the corner in the most eloquent terms. 'I'm tellin' ya, Nigel. He's dropped his fuckin' bollocks, I'm tellin' ya!'

Sanders chips in: 'He's gone, Nigel, he's fuckin' gone!'

Again. Not quite. But it would not be long.

Round Nine   *Just Another Cigarette*

Albert: 'We're into uncharted territory for Gerald McClellan. He's never been past round eight in his entire career.'

   Pacheco: 'But he's got a sinkin' battleship in front of him. All he needs to do is finish. Benn is on the way and sinking. But he's got heart. Great energy, great heart from Benn. Boy, he's halfway out this fight and he's still in there tryin' to finish.'

   Benn is punching on instinct now. Hitting air. Sweated-up eyes, all red and blazing. Every fibre soaked. From the soles of his boots to the tips of his dreadlocks, he is a molten mess of anger. A long right lands. Two behind the ear. Gerald holds on.

   Pacheco: 'McClellan again with that fatal flaw, waiting too long. He should be all over this guy with a methodical attack.'

   Gerald retreats. Nigel scores with another long right. Two more behind the ear. He's on top. No way back for McClellan now.

   And then . . .

   Benn hurls a right, discus-style. Loses balance. He clips McClellan with the knotted beads of his dreads and bangs his forehead on Gerald's cheek as he swings himself off his feet and lands on the canvas. Gerald paws at his face where Nigel's hair made contact. He's distressed. Confused. As Benn gets up, panting and desperate in centre ring, McClellan signals to Asaro that something is wrong and goes down on one knee in Benn's corner. Sanders is standing right behind him, peering through the ropes at the stricken man. Only an hour before, they had chatted amicably in Gerald's dressing room, when Sanders came in to check the wrapping on his hands. 'We'll have dinner later,' McClellan had said. They went back a few years. Lot to talk about. Not now. Sanders can only be hoping Gerald does not choose to get up. Not so.

   Pacheco: 'He got butted on the way down.'

   Albert: 'Oh boy! Oh boy! McClellan will have time to . . . but the referee says, "Get up". Now here we go. Round nine continues.'

   Pacheco: 'That was no kinda knockdown. He got butted real hard.'

McClellan gets up. Back to the familiar hell of the fight. Nigel belts him on the back of the head again. Asaro warns him.

Pacheco is losing patience with McClellan. 'He's waiting too long. He's waiting too long.'

It has been obvious for several rounds that there is something seriously wrong with the American. From somewhere, though, he finds a right, a left to the ribs. His practised winning shots. The ones from Milwaukee. Old favourites. Drags them up from his memory and lets them go. Some dog.

Ferdie, meanwhile, marvels that Benn is still there. 'It's a miracle he's still up. He can't control his legs. Can't get 'em in the right position.'

Albert agrees. 'That last flurry in the eighth round really took the steam out of Nigel Benn, when he went down.'

Only now did it dawn on me that we were watching two men careering towards the ultimate sacrifice. This had not been a prospect I had dwelt on in any of the previous rounds. To this point, it had been a collision of undeniable intensity, perhaps the 'best fight' most of us there had ever seen live, but contests between two dangerous punchers such as these invariably end in a countout, negating the possibility of death. Here in the ninth, however, doom cloaked the night. It was as if it had gone too far and nobody could do anything about it. The finish fight the crowd secretly craved was now a real possibility. Our own inner fight was with our guilt.

It seemed at the time – as it did subsequently – that McClellan was in the greater trouble. It also looked as if he were aware of his predicament. Benn, on the other hand, was hurting physically but his head, although constantly pounded, was clear enough for him to navigate his way through this terrifying jungle of pain. His brain was in place.

At ringside, we had the luxury of reflection, however brief, and could wonder about the morality of seeing Benn and McClellan risk dying for money and a title while we watched. There are moralists who will say that is a question we should be asking before rather than during a fight. But we don't. We surrender to our weaknesses.

If there is any morality in boxing, it surely resides inside the ring.

That is where the honesty is. Elsewhere, in words and contracts and skullduggery, lies the profound sinning. En route to this book, I had reason to believe that more strongly than ever ...

It was just another cigarette. One afternoon in Miami, in the summer of '61 in the Fifth Street gym, it was dangling, unlit and nondescript, from the bottom lip of Hank Kaplan. Hank, one of boxing's celebrity gym rats, had the ear of the game's best-informed practitioners. Probably still does ...

... There I am, then, thirty-nine years later, having a drink with a friend in Graziano's bar in Canastota, five and a half hours west of New York City. A white guy with a flat nose, about fifty or so, insinuates himself into our conversation in the gloom of the bar, slips me a little card with an old fight picture of Carl 'Bobo' Olson on it. He is in fight pose, gloved up for the camera. 'Saw you talking to Hank,' says the stranger, a Vietnam vet with a stiffened right hand. He used to box. Now he trains. And, like Hank, he trades in memorabilia. The traders in tat were in Canastota in good numbers, using the induction ceremony at the International Boxing Hall of Fame as an appropriate marketplace for their wares.

'Keep it. Could be worth a lot of money one day.'

Never met Hank Kaplan in my life, as far as I know. Didn't know this guy either. But they were both trawling the stalls. Anyway, I had no interest in buying paper bits of a broken fighter. Especially not Bobo. Half an hour earlier, he was sitting on a stage under a tent in a nearby field, propped up by his sons and staring into space occupied by those who'd come to enshrine him in the hall of fame. Olson, a good Hawaiian middleweight in the fifties, a world champion, is nearly gone. Alzheimer's.

I look at this tough-talking vet with wounded eyes, a decent man most likely, who might have known no better. He trained a fighter, waiting for the right fight. Then perhaps they'd break into the big time. If not, he'd let him go. This is the culture of using he has grown up with.

We finish our drinks and our conversation. I look at the tatty old picture of Bobo. And I remember Hank's cigarette ...

*

Among those knowing types back in '61 in Miami was Chris Dundee. Mr Dundee it was who had invited Mr Kaplan down to the gym to cast his eye over a young fighter being trained by his brother Angelo.

That cigarette never got lit. Before Hank could put flame to it, Angelo's prodigy, a breezy character whose hand speed matched his own outrageous boasts, had whipped it from his lip. Cassius Clay took a pen and, with a right hand accustomed to more percussive activity, scribbled a childlike signature along the cigarette's thin paper case. He did it delicately and neatly, so as not to punch the nib into the tobacco. Cassius suspected Hank would thank him for his dexterity one day.

The first time I saw a picture of the cigarette was on page 33 in a catalogue that came my way a few years ago: 'Christie's Los Angeles, The Paloger Collection of Muhammad Ali Memorabilia, Sunday, 19 October 1997.' The cigarette was for sale, along with thousands of other Ali items. The husbanding of that little piece of boxing detritus for thirty-six years might be a metaphor for the sport. The cigarette's intrinsic value was, say, the slimmest percentage of a penny. Yet, dressed up by a famous hand, this humble cigarette was set upon a most unusual journey to celebrity. It says something about boxing that the cigarette is in better shape than Muhammad. The unspoken contract entered into between Clay and Kaplan in 1961 was that everything is for sale in the fight game. Everything from a thirty-six-year-old cigarette to credibility. Christie's wanted between $800 and $1,200 for it.

Even if he has resurrected himself as a worldwide personality and single-handedly reignited the Ali industry to the point of overkill, Ali is the most visible victim of the exploitation that is boxing's curse. Where he differs from most other old pugs is in his ability to reinvent himself at a good price. Ali charges $100,000 each public appearance. Appearance? It's almost an apparition. He appears but says nothing that can be heard. Of the estimated 10,000 professional boxers at work around the world, maybe 10 per cent will earn something near their worth over an average career of a decade or so. The rest will not get the breaks or the money, often because they're just not good enough. When it is over, their worth will be calculated in pennies not millions.

And yet it is a multibillion-dollar industry. Promoters and television executives are not on benefit too often, or abandoned as human wreckage in a cheap hotel room, like Heenan – or, in more recent times, those fine fighters Jimmy Bivins and Sandy Saddler. Jimmy, cleaned up and smiling, was at Canastota too. There were sightings of Sandy in the Bronx about the same time, but nobody tracked him down.

Writing this book, I had a search of my own. I'd finally located Stan Johnson in Los Angeles – in unusual circumstances. He was training his forty-eight-year-old sister Margerie, who had a serious drug problem, to fight Muhammad Ali's daughter Laila, and we collided at the weigh-in. Farce was a word never too far from this promotion but, to Stan, it was just another gig. Margerie too.

I couldn't help thinking this was a major breach of faith in a sibling, throwing her in against someone young enough to be her daughter. But, as Al Moreland said, Stan had long reconciled winning and losing in boxing. This was just an engagement, a job of work. If Margerie could get through it in reasonable shape, what's the problem?

She'd only got the fight, anyway, because her son's girlfriend had turned down the purse. It was said to be little more than $500, less than Christie's were asking for Hank's famous cigarette. Laila got $50,000.

This really was the top and the bottom of the 'baahxin' bizness'.

I could only feel sorry for Margerie. Whatever they'd been dealt in life, they were surviving the best they could. Margerie might have been a wild mother, but she wasn't totally stupid. She knew what she was supposed to do against Laila. She liked the girl. Reckoned she'd got a big future. 'Not like that for me, though,' Margerie said. 'I ain't tryin' to do what Laila do. I ain't no for-real boxer. I know why I'm here.'

Margerie, who only took up fighting in the ring a couple of years earlier 'to deal with all sorts of shit', reckoned she was pretty handy in a street fight. I believed her. Come the night, at the Universal Amphitheatre, she was a long way from the street. She shot some weak jabs over Laila's head and took her licks – a left hook, right cross, down twice, all over in a round. Beaten, she leaned over the ropes and gave Laila's dad a big wink. He was more her age, anyway.

The *Los Angeles Times* went out on a limb. It described it as possibly the worst fight in the history of fighting.

What did Laila care? She was heading for a big-money showdown with Jacqui Frazier-Lyde, daughter of you-know-who. Joe was at ringside too. Sitting in Muhammad's shadow as usual.

I wondered if Laila would be interested in raising some money for Gerald. I could get a film crew together and do a documentary of her fight with Jacqui, with some of the proceeds going into McClellan's trust fund. I put the idea to her manager, Johnny 'Yahyah' McClain, who would soon become her husband. We offered him $60,000 for access. All he and Laila would have to do would be to talk to camera occasionally. We'd be their fly on the wall. He wanted $100,000 – plus $100,000 for the Fraziers. I wasn't sure how he got to negotiate on behalf of the other party. But the money was ridiculous anyway. We called it off.

It was a wasted opportunity. Joe is a friend of Gerald's and has visited him many times in Freeport. He was up for it. Ali regularly sends Gerald cards. They even tried to speak on the phone once. Ali barely able to raise a whisper, Gerald unable to hear him anyway.

Watt: 'This is good news for Benn, good news for Benn. McClellan doesn't like it.'

Gutteridge: 'Benn always said if he gets in a distance thing with this guy he'll find out if he's got it.'

Watt: 'There's a question mark hanging over McClellan now, Reg.'

McClellan's boxing has lost all shape. Benn is bullying him into a ragged brawl, as he has done for most of the fight. Gerald can only grab, hold and swing when his arms are free.

Watt: 'McClellan's strength is not in his uppercuts, it is in his straight rights and his hooks. When Benn gets in close and low he has very little to fear. McClellan does not use uppercuts very often.'

It is an astute analysis. The way to defuse a power puncher is to rob him of his leverage and space. It puts him out of a rhythm. Unable to get set, he finds himself being dictated to rather than fighting his own fight. McClellan had long since surrendered the initiative, although he'd had his moments in the eighth. Now he knew he was being hustled out of the fight.

End of the round.

Pacheco observes, 'Gerald's blinking his eyes. He got hit hard.'

He certainly got hit hard. All night, he got hit hard. All his life, he got hit hard. In the corner, he looks out past Stan, hears him say, 'You can't lose this fight. You're too far ahead. They said you couldn't go ten. You already got there. He cannot win this fight unless you give this fight to him.'

Across the ring, Mancini says to Benn, 'His arsehole went in that round, Nigel. But don't forget the jab. Now come on. Three rounds to go, Nigel. Just three rounds to go.'

They'd gone nine. McClellan would not finish the tenth.

12

Round Ten   *'Un! Deux! Trois! Quatre! Cinq! Six!*
Sept! Huit! Neuf! Dix!'

Albert: 'Nigel Benn hoping that he got a second wind between rounds . . . A left hand by McClellan!'

Pacheco: 'The only way McClellan can lose this fight . . . well, he can lose it many ways . . . but one way he can lose it is to be cautious and not fight ten, eleven and twelve rounds. He can't give it away. He's gotta fight.'

Albert: 'A confident Gerald McClellan. Benn just looking to hang on.'

Nigel lands another heavy right. McClellan is in serious trouble. That right has spun him into another zone. He is the one hanging on. It all starts to untangle now, halfway into the tenth. Nigel sweeps a right over the top of Gerald's injured head. Gerald goes down on his right knee. He rests his left glove on his other knee. He looks up at Asaro, who is counting. In French. 'Un! Deux!'

Time slows. Light is everywhere. McClellan is alone in a public place. Yet he is strangely serene. Relaxed, almost composed.

'Trois! Quatre!'

Pacheco: 'Gotta get up.'

'Cinq! Six!'

Pacheco: 'Now that is the strangest knockdown I've seen.'

Gerald gets up at seven. Walks into Asaro. Holds his gloves out. The referee looks at them, rubs them on the fighter's shorts. Lets him loose. Gerald's eyelids are working hard now, like a butterfly in a storm.

Nigel speeds another right on to the top and back of Gerald's head.

Albert: 'Everybody's on their feet, 11,000-strong!'

Benn shoots an uppercut, then a short, stiff right. Every punch is zeroing in on the danger area around the temple. McClellan is gone. He takes another half-blow and goes on that vertical slide, like an elevator smoothly travelling to the basement. He comes to rest on his right knee. Strikes the same pose as only seconds before. As does Asaro. With one minute and thirty-five seconds left in the round, the referee starts to count again.

'Un! Deux!'

It is done without ceremony or emotion. This is Asaro's role.

'Trois!'

Benn walks to a neutral corner, casually, like Joe Louis used to do. Like Joe, Nigel is used to seeing men fall before him. Except Gerald is kneeling. Waiting for something to descend around his shoulders, a veil of light.

'Quatre! Cinq!'

But the young American, getting older by the second, is not easy with the time-out this time. There is no peace in it. His body is shutting down. He blinks, gasps, gulps in the air. First time, he looked up at Asaro. Now he looks only at the canvas. Asaro has nothing to communicate to him now, nor has Gerald anything left to say. He just has to wait.

'Six! Sept!'

Asaro uses both hands, all ten fingers, palms facing his own chest. He is shouting at McClellan. Gerald will wait until Asaro has stopped shouting before he moves again.

Benn shifts in from the corner a couple of feet to have a closer look at his prey, thin legs boyishly balancing a fighting man's body. His gloved hands are still coiled in tension. He's counting too. He counts and hopes. He hopes Gerald will not get up. If he does, he has work left to do. If he doesn't, the roof is going to blow. Everybody in the building is counting. The world has gone into super slo-mo. The noise has ebbed. Maybe a yard from McClellan, I can see the figure of Don King in his dinner jacket, standing, two hands resting on the ring apron, and screaming at his man. I turn my head slowly back to McClellan, a half-naked, totally defeated fighter.

'Huit! Neuf! Dix!'

Asaro crosses his arms and waves them in the accepted manner. It's over.

In a frozen moment, McClellan's right knee lifts from the canvas, Benn's knees dip, he spreads his arms wide, accepting the embrace of the crowd.

The whole room goes out of control. Inside the ropes, the canvas is covered instantly in expensive, shiny shoes. Fat rich men jostle for the spotlight vacated by the fighters; outside, row upon row of the mob move and shout as one. They high-five and laugh the smile-free laugh of the cruel voyeur. They are drunk on violent conclusion. They have thrown their last inner punch and they will soon be deflated.

The energy in the ring has travelled through the night like electricity to the crowd, who, collectively, could probably provide the material for a very

Benn, spent and hopeful, watches from a neutral corner as the French referee, Alfred Asaro, brings McClellan's fighting days to an end. © Dan Smith.

acceptable orgy or riot, so high are they. This is what they paid for, this is why they came to Docklands when they could have watched the fight at home on television. This is why we fight and why we watch others who fight. At the moment of victory, you do not have to ask the question. In fact, the question is never asked. We just know.

The mob is at one with Benn. The champion's eyes roll, he screams with the wild joy of the conqueror . . .

Albert: 'Nigel Benn has won!'

Pacheco: 'I can't believe that!'

Albert: 'One of the most bizarre endings to a fight. One of the most compelling fight nights you'll ever see!'

Benn went up on to the second strand of the ropes, in his own corner. This was the place he'd gone back to nine times, after each round of scheduled torture. Now it was his place of celebration. He was waving his right glove at the crowd. There was anger, retribution and a fierce kind of happiness on his face. He screamed – but at nobody in particular. He'd shown us. Like Ali. He'd proved them wrong. He shook up the world.

And now, without turning away from the darkness, Benn pointed his glove dismissively in the direction of the spent challenger, whom he could not see because of the enveloping confusion in the ring. Stan and Donnie were wiping Gerald down – there was only blank resignation on the beaten man's bruised features. And, from where I sat, what looked like the cold fear of resignation.

Fighters can hate each other, physically, for half an hour or so, and then they're as close as is possible outside romance. But Nigel didn't move towards Gerald's corner, as convention dictates. There would be no ritual hug here. No warrior recognition. Nigel was in his own zone.

What I did not see during his celebration was a hint of a smile. His body message was triumph in battle, without a peace treaty. It was ugly and it was beautiful. He'd overcome. He was Superman.

Gary Newbon approached him with his ITV microphone. Benn set himself for another confrontation. He was still high on the fight, and he would stretch the joy of victory as far as it would go.

Scientists have recently discovered that the winner in a fight has hypertestosterone levels, while the loser's testosterone count drops. Darwin would have argued this prepares the winner for mating, and saves the vanquished from himself, reducing his will to fight, so that he will withdraw, perhaps to fight again later.

Benn might have been ready to mate, but he was extending no fraternal warmth to the man in the suit coming towards him. Newbon was in a sweat. He'd had his post-fight interview rows with Benn before, but it wasn't that which concerned him. It was the general air of confusion, and the plight of McClellan. The uncontrolled shouting and general shoving was not helped by King's superactive sidekick, Mike Marley. Marley, a former New York boxing writer who had crossed over to the promotion side, was waving his hands about, pointing to TV people, to journalists, to trainers and various hangers-on. King stood about with a slightly comical regal air, waiting, as ever, to be interviewed. He occasionally looked towards McClellan's corner. Frank Warren was in the ring too, and subdued. He could see that McClellan was badly hurt.

Newbon tried to calm Benn, to capture the excitement of the event with dignity. The TV clock was running down. Newbon had to ask his questions before the ads kicked in. He started to tell Benn how great he was, how he'd defied the odds. He wanted him to listen then respond with a few appropriate soundbites, as is the deal when TV is paying the freight. But Benn doesn't do soundbites or platitudes.

'Nigel,' Newbon began, 'that was not only your greatest performance, that was one of the greatest boxing performances of all time in this country.'

'Yeah, well, all you lot were geeing him up, giving it this, giving it that. I knew he wouldn't be able to go the distance . . .'

Benn, never looking at Newbon, broke off to wave his still-gloved fist again at the simmering crowd. 'Yeah!' he shouted.

'But Nigel . . .'

'No, no, you listen to me! I'd like to thank my trainer, Kevin Sanders. Everyone sayin' we ain't goin' anywhere without Jimmy Tibbs. Proved him wrong. And not only that, the person I'd like to thank most of all is Paul McKenna, who hypnotised me and made me believe in myself.'

Newbon, fearing a roll-call of everyone Benn had ever known in boxing, tried again to ask another question. Nigel would not be silenced.

'No, no. You listen to me. I'm always listenin' to you.'

They came to a muddled compromise and Newbon attempted to talk Benn through some highlights. But Gary started to lose it. As he swung around towards McClellan's corner, he said, 'Mike McCallum's actually very badly hurt and they've got a stretcher in here, Nigel. I'm sorry. Mike McClellan. Gerald McClellan. Sorry. I'm getting confused here.'

It was all unravelling. Mike McCallum, the world-class middleweight, had fought on the undercard. Newbon, who had his producer yelling corrections down his earpiece, motioned Benn away from McClellan's corner, where they'd been standing. And still there was no sensible dialogue between fighter and interviewer.

Out of the corner of his eye, Newbon had seen that McClellan had slipped from his stool and was lying on his back. His producer told him to get on with the interview and Newbon looked towards the board doctor to see if it was all right to continue. 'Gary!' shouted his producer. 'Get on with it!'

Benn had either not heard Newbon telling him about McClellan or had ignored it. 'No, mate. They only brought him over to bash me up, mate. I'm gonna say what I want to say. Let me tell you that now. They only brought him in to bash me up, mate. No chance ... no chance ... no chance ...'

Benn was oblivious to everything and everyone, including McClellan. He only wanted to talk about the fight. At that moment in his life, it was his courage and his victory that defined him. He would allow nothing to intrude on that. 'I don't care if you knock me down, I was ready to go with him. Whatever he wanted to, I was going to match him. All the way, mate. All the way. Now you might start believin' in the Dark Destroyer. I'm number one. Second to no one!'

Benn's eyes had dimmed from wild to steady. Trance-like, even.

He was still darting hard glances around the ring, only half-listening to Newbon, who had tried to signal to his production people to finish the interview as the ring descended into unmendable chaos.

'We're going to wrap this interview here, Jim, because we've got a serious problem with Gerald McClellan.'

Newbon was hoping the director would pan back for a final summing-up from Jim Rosenthal. The show had gone on long enough for Newbon. He was visibly affected by the fight and by Benn's responses and McClellan's collapse.

'It was terrible,' Newbon said later. 'My director wasn't really aware. Not his fault. So I'm saying, "This is serious, this is really serious." Everyone got a bit het-up and then we all realised there was a problem. We went into long-shot to get off the air.'

Benn turned away without ceremony. King touched his gloves in a gesture of congratulation, but Benn was not going to be soft-soaped by the promoter he reckoned had wanted him beaten.

Rosenthal, up in the gantry, wound it all down and the credits rolled over some of the key action as a night of drama was brought to a clinical close. McClellan was still lying in his corner. The medics had gathered and the ambulance driver had his engine running outside the arena.

'Concern is spreading around this arena,' concluded Rosenthal. 'It's been a wonderful performance by this fella. You can't take it away from him. What Nigel Benn has done here tonight, he has proved everybody wrong. And he has done it showing unbelievable fighting heart. He's done it. What a fight. Nigel Benn. Bye-bye.'

It was coming up to midnight. After ITV had gone home, Showtime stayed on. Their overhead camera showed McClellan still on his back in his corner, and Steve Albert commented, 'Our prayers are with Gerald McClellan,' before handing over to Ferdie Pacheco and Benn.

Pacheco had no more luck than Newbon in directing Benn's attention towards McClellan's plight. There was more of 'no, no, mate, you listen to me' from Benn, who wanted to look forward, not sideways or back. Speaking to an American audience now, he called out the best twelve-stone fighter in the world, Roy Jones Jr, the man Gerald had beaten as an amateur, the man Gerald hoped to beat as a professional. That would prove how good he was, said Benn. Jones was the new benchmark.

King hove into view again. He said the doctors were doing a magnificent job on Gerald and hoped everything would be OK. Pacheco struggled to put things in context. But boxing beat him. The hype was in. The adrenalin flowed over everyone in the ring. There was no emotional space left for McClellan.

The Sunday writers were in a state of calm agitation. It's like emergency surgery: you have a body, a fault and a few minutes to fix it. A bum diagnosis in print and you can look stupid. Caveats are slipped in early: 'Doctors were quickly at McClellan's side ...', 'His corner looked worried but ringside officials said he was being taken to hospital without delay . . .' These are journalistic insurance policies. Gamble on a prognosis – a real temptation – and you can put a fighter on the critical list when he's up and walking around next day, with your name on a story about his life-threatening injuries.

I was shouting down the phone to a copy-taker who had watched the fight on television back in the *Observer* office. She was as professional as ever in taking down my version of events but stopped me at one point to enquire about McClellan's condition. I told her he was still lying in his corner but the doctors were around him and doing the best they could. Describing the fight seemed obscene alongside this central concern of the evening. The copy-taker knew what the real story was, but I had an obligation to describe how we had reached this point. There were punches and knockdowns to talk about, an analysis to be made, perhaps grab a quote.

It all seemed so surreal, as it had done when I'd been in such situations before. What can it matter, the result of an arranged fight between two strangers, when one of them might die in front of us as we write our paltry words? I tried as best I could to stay calm, to imagine what the words would look like in the following morning's *Observer*, after the chaos had subsided. After Gerald had faced death.

At the time, I saw it this way:

Nigel Benn wanted a war. Quite whether the World Boxing Council super-middleweight champion wanted collateral damage of these proportions is doubtful.

Gerald McClellan, who brought as much menace to his challenge as he relishes in his pit bull dogs at home in Illinois, was carried from the ring on a stretcher, his neck in a brace, with anxious doctors feeding him oxygen after 10 of the most brutal rounds seen in a British ring for many years.

But, for all the blood-lust that was welling in the capacity audience of 10,300 for more than half an hour, boxing could not stand too much of this on a regular basis. McClellan, never stopped in 33 fights and a fierce puncher himself, was 'talking and lucid' in the Royal London Hospital, Whitechapel, according to the ringside doctor, Ossie Ross. Lying alongside him in the next cubicle was Benn, who had collapsed in his dressing room from hyperventilation. No sport should demand this sort of commitment, or these consequences, from any man.

But boxing does. And boxers give it. Abolitionists will howl again, the squeamish will turn away and blind defenders of the faith will call it 'unfortunate'. And unfortunate it is that one man at ringside does not have the powers of expression any more to give us his feelings on the matter.

Michael Watson, disabled since his fight against Chris Eubank in 1991, is a friend of Benn's and undoubtedly wishes both of last night's combatants the very best. But it is extraordinary that he can even bring himself to watch boxing any more – especially since the death last year of the young east Londoner, Bradley Stone. The reality is that, for all protestations to the contrary, most of the people who come to rings and halls around the country want exactly what they saw last night. When the entertainment turns sour, however, they move quietly away from the fire that our own primal urgings continue to kindle.

Some, though, cannot get enough.

As Gerald was being eased into the ambulance, most of the punters were filing out the exits, sated, dazed and looking for a drink or a cab. They were hoarse from screaming. Intoxicated in a draining way. They had come to see a proper tear-up and they'd got one. But they would have liked it to be cleaner. Nobody likes to see a fighter carried from the ring. Except maybe the psycho-pathic few. And there are always some of them. As the ambulance engine roared into life, and Donnie and Stan held Gerald's now-retired fists, the echo of leather could just be heard in the arena behind them.

Back in the ring that housed McClellan's awful farewell to fight-ing, a walkout six-rounder was working its way to a fierce conclu-sion. A supporter of one of the combatants, a popular north London banger, screamed hatefully: 'Kill him! Put him in hospital like the fucking Yank!'

McClellan knew that language. Earlier in the week he said, 'When I'm in the ring with another fighter, I look across the ring and see this guy I have so much hate for. I have so much desire to knock this guy unconscious.'

Showtime's cameras were still rolling and Ferdie Pacheco, the Fight Doctor, was giving his prognosis. If anyone should know about the dangers of the boxing business it is the doctor who was at Muhammad Ali's side for much of his career. Introduced to Ali by Angelo Dundee, around the corner from his medical practice in Miami in 1962, Pacheco saw Ali disintegrate but was powerless to help. Ali would not be told.

But Ferdie was in the boxing business. There was no place for sentiment. He felt human compassion for McClellan, naturally, but he spoke about his performance, most specifically his surrender, in derisory terms.

Rolling the replay tape, Ferdie opined that he could not remem-ber a champ quitting like this. Just going down on one knee and not getting up. But how did he think that was much different from not coming out for the eleventh round, the option a shellacked Ali was forced to accept in his penultimate fight, against Larry Holmes? Was it substantially different either from Joe Frazier being pulled out at the end of the fourteenth by Eddie Futch, in the Thrilla in Manila? Did he not now remember, as Ali looked over at Joe in that minute before the scheduled final round, that the winner that night also wanted to quit?

He might have forgotten one or two others. Ray Mercer cracked Francesco Damiani's nose in half once and the Italian sensibly pulled out. Later, Ferdie and the rest of us would witness Tyson turn away from Holyfield. Plenty of fighters have quit. It's just how you call it. Quit is the dirtiest word in boxing. But in every fight, one fighter ultimately has to admit, to himself first, that he can suffer no more, that the other guy is the better man. He might not be able to put it into words, he might deny it until he dies. But he knows. He knows that if they'd let it go on, he'd have to quit in the end, one way or another. Because the only alternative is self-destruction.

'We didn't see a punch that was worthy,' Pacheco said to Steve Albert. 'That one went over his head. That was like a voluntary, like, "I think I'm quittin'."'

Benn was seen to crack McClellan with a powerful right flush on the side of the head. By any standards it was a major blow. A lot of fighters would have toppled. The Doctor had to concede, 'Now that was heavy. That was heavy. Could be that punch way back then that did it to him, but . . .' And then: 'Here comes the second [knockdown], the resignation, coz his eyes were wide open. There was no reason for him to go down.'

We can't have been watching the same tape. Benn's right homed in again, sending a spray of sweat several feet. Pacheco said, 'There's no big, effective punch that puts him down. Absolute resignation. That's all.'

Ferdie wanted closure. Satisfying, tidy finality. A clean, unmistakable conclusion. A story with an end we can understand. Not a mystery. We want it done properly. We want a finished fight because it is a war. We don't want a count. We want the loser to lose as losers used to lose. On their back, or face down. It doesn't matter. We want a K-N-O-C-K-O-U-T!

The American cameras would shut down soon, too. They'd wrap it up back in the States, express concern for McClellan, roll their credits and go home. Several hours later, they would show the fight to an American audience, time-delayed. Like a clever stop-counter jab, one of the sneakiest punches in boxing.

On the way to the hospital, McClellan comes round in the ambulance and rips off the oxygen mask. Disorientated but briefly revived, he says to Johnson, 'What the fuck happen? I got knocked clean out, didn't I?'

Johnson squeezes Gerald's hand and tells him what he does not want to hear: 'No, man. You didn't get knocked out. You went down to one knee and you walked back to the corner and you quit.' This is the cold professional boxing assessment. Technically, it is accurate. McClellan refuses to believe it. He turns to Donnie and says, 'Donnie, you tell this motherfucker he lyin' to me, ain't he!' Donnie shakes his moonface from side to side and answers, 'No, G-Man, that's exactly what happen.'

In a little while, as the resident neurosurgeon Mr Sutcliffe and the staff at the Royal London Hospital begin preparing to save Gerald's life, Nigel Benn is wheeled into the cubicle next to him. He gets up, kisses Gerald's hand and says, 'Sorry.' Except Stan said later he never heard Nigel say that.

He heard something else, though.

Don King arrived soon after Benn to see the man who had been his fighter, the product he hoped would generate big money against Roy Jones, the fighter Benn said he'd brought over 'to bash me up', but who would now definitely not play any further part in King's plans.

Standing not far from Gerald's bed, Don turned to Stan and Donnie and said, 'Gerald quit, man . . . He quit like a dog.'

Some dog.

13

Après le Deluge

About this time at another hospital, thousands of miles away in Freeport, another McClellan, Lisa, was finishing up her shift as a trainee nurse. She was getting ready to go home to her place on the east side of town. There she would clean up a little, call a few friends and get ready to watch her brother's big fight. A hard-core boxing fan, she reckoned Gerald would win. Easy. Within an hour, that tranquil certainty would be disturbed by a phone call from London . . .

A friend of Gerald's, a Freeport real-estate agent called Edgar Oppenheimer, was getting ready to watch the fight too. About half an hour before the telecast, 9 p.m. local time, he rang Gerald's girlfriend, Angie Brown, to say hello. Edgar didn't know the result. Angie did. She said, 'Edgar, I can't talk to you right now. I got to get ready to go to London. Gerald's been badly hurt.'

'Holy Christmas! I'm real sorry, Angie. Let you go.' He turned to his wife, who was also settling down to watch, and said, 'Apparently Gerald gets hurt in this fight.' It was a weird suspension of time and reality. Edgar reckons Showtime said nothing about Gerald's condition before they put the fight out. There was no news on the radio. Or the TV news. The only link to Gerald's bedside was the telephone, with Donnie on one end and the family on the other.

Lisa recalls, 'We were all prepared to go over Stacey's to watch the fight. And, I was on my way outta the door to go to the store, and . . . my other sister Sandra called and she said that Gerald . . . and Donnie, he'd called from the hospital . . . he'd told Sand that Gerald got knocked out, but he was fine . . . see so many different stories . . . he got knocked, he was fine, they was takin' him to the hospital for observation.'

Separated from their injured brother by time, distance and a cousin who was going into panic overload, the McClellans could only wait for the next phone call.

Donnie told Lisa the whole story, as much as he could keep it all together. It was a nightmare phone call. Donnie was scared. Shortly after his first call, he got back on the phone. 'Gerald's slipped into a coma. We got five minutes to make a decision or he's gonna die.'

There was really no choice. Donnie told the surgeon to do what he had to do. Mr Sutcliffe induced a coma to calm the brain, cut a hole in Gerald's head and eased the pressure building up between brain and skull that threatened to kill Gerald. He did this sort of operation maybe twenty times a week, mainly on car accident victims. He was widely regarded as one of the best surgeons in his field. Gerald was in excellent hands and had been delivered to Mr Sutcliffe with as much efficiency as boxing's new safety regulations could ensure.

It was Michael Watson's accident four years earlier that had forced the British Boxing Board of Control into another bout of introspection. The death in 1994 of Bradley Stone hastened the introduction of the new measures, which called for ringside anaesthetists and an ambulance to be waiting outside the building. The promoters had taken the precaution of providing two ambulances. It was always going to be a two-ambulance fight.

Once Gerald had been operated on, the medical staff at the Royal London Hospital could do little but watch and wait. Mr Sutcliffe advised the family that it would be in his best interests if he stayed in London for as long as possible. Lisa, for one, was not happy with that arrangement.

In the days and weeks after the fight, the world went about its business without Gerald. In the weeks leading up to the fight, there might well have been a million words spent on it. Maybe a hundred hours of TV. Radio too. The accreditation desk hummed with activity. Celebrities were on the phone for free tickets. The punters salivated and queued. The promoters, the fighters, the managers – anyone connected with the show – were keen to talk. Benn was even chided for not talking enough. He was not 'doing his bit' to sell tickets, said Frank Warren.

And then came the fight, the roar of disgust and the black hole of indifference. It is always the same.

Gerald got shuffled down the news list. Concern for beaten boxers after a fight fades like a slice of cold moon. The columnists columnise. The doctors fulminate. Politicians blow hard. Fighters go quiet ... and the customers, at home and in the auditorium, pay little heed to the debate. Until the next time.

Within four days the story was reduced to three paragraphs in *The Times*. Eleven days after the fight, McClellan rated a five-par mention by the Associated Press when he came off his life-support machine. 'He's doing quite well,' Mr Sutcliffe said. 'He's starting to wake up. He's breathing for himself. He's opening his eyes and starting to move. He's one step removed from critical. He's stable, but he's still not out of danger.'

One week after Benn–McClellan, Naseem Hamed appeared on the last significant terrestrial fight on British television for about five years. After days of widely reported concern about the viability of boxing, with Gerald still unconscious in hospital, it was an obviously sensitive situation. As Srikumar Sen said in *The Times*, 'However distasteful it may be to some to see another young man crashing on to their living-room floor, business is business and there is no business like the boxing business.' Frank Warren asked Hamed to keep his entrance dignified. Ingle, Hamed's trainer at the time, responded with no sense of comic intent, 'He will just do his somersault and no more.' Ingle added, 'It's like going on the production line in a factory and slowing down; you are going to get the sack. Let's not have all this hypocrisy. It's a job, like any other job. Naz's job is to get him out of there just as soon as possible.' Inside two rounds, Hamed knocked unconscious the ill-equipped Argentine Sergio Liendo, a knockout he still regards as his most satisfying.

Six weeks after the fight McClellan went home, flown out by the promoters. Mr Sutcliffe wanted him to stay a little longer, to let the treatment stabilise. He said it would give McClellan the best chance of a good recovery. But the family wanted him home. It was their call, for better or worse.

On 4 April, not long after McClellan had been admitted to the University of Michigan Hospital in Ann Arbor, Jim Callaghan, the

Member for Heywood and Middleton (not to be confused with the former Labour Prime Minister), put forward a bill in the House of Commons to ban boxing. He said 361 boxers had died in the ring, worldwide, since 1945. He'd been a sports teacher when younger, but 'always had doubts about the merits of boxing'.

Mr Callaghan mentioned Gerald's pre-fight declaration of intent, although he too misquoted it: 'You have to go to war and in war you have to be prepared to die.'

Mr Callaghan continued: 'That is what boxing is. We all know that Gerald got his war, and that, tragically, he paid the price in his savage bout with Nigel Benn. I am sure that I speak for all Honourable Members in the House today in saying that we all wish him well now that he has survived a life-threatening injury and been flown back to the United States of America to be with his family.'

It was heartfelt, solidly argued and predictable. The motion failed. Like several previous attempts and, almost certainly, like the next one, and the one after that.

Boxing does not welcome outsiders. It settles its differences in its own way. The row raging around Gerald would not have the benefit of legislators' wisdom or even the stamp of a court. It would be an ugly and inconclusive affair. Business as usual.

14

Too Much Monkey Business

Gerald eventually made it home to Wyandotte Street six months after being carried from the ring in London. They'd moved him out of Ann Arbor and into a hospital in Milwaukee, where Lisa said he received excellent treatment and attention.

In November, Gerald's auntie, Linda Shorter, was made his official guardian. Linda, the sister of Gerald's mother Genola, had some job on her hands. Genola's drinking disbarred her, and the daughters resisted attempts by their father Emmite to supervise Gerald's affairs because they suspected he had been bought off by Don King.

One reason they doubted Emmite's sincerity was that he changed his story about the fight contract. During the hearing, Emmite claimed he knew Gerald was supposed to fight for $450,000. 'When Gerald got hurt, Don King took the original contract back and ran a phoney contract on him,' he alleged. (This, says Johnson, is why King wanted himself and Donnie out of London.) Emmite said King had someone take the contract from Gerald's room while he was hospitalised in London. Later he said he'd never seen the contract but that Manny Steward told him the purse should have been $450,000.

As the father wriggled, the sisters fumed. They reckoned King had got to their father. King denied it. So did Emmite. He left town for a while.

And around Gerald's stricken body, the able-bodied squared off again. This was the money fight.

In January of '96, Frank Warren produced accounts on behalf of himself and King, in response to Lisa's repeated claims that Gerald had been ripped off. King had refused to show anyone the fight contract, and the volume was being turned up.

The promoters said Gerald was paid a total of $250,215.37 for the fight, with no deductions. The figure comprised a purse of $200,000, the balance, $50,215.37, being described as training expenses, a regular practice in boxing.

On top of that, Warren said, Gerald and his family received another $259,722.50, made up of post-fight medical and travel expenses, as well as a payment to Emanuel Steward and John Davimos, who had previously handled Gerald's career. Gerald and his family received a total of $508,494, said Warren.

These are the accounts of all the monies Gerald should have received:

Air ambulance	$90,443.25
Hotel bills, air fares for family	$50,000.00 (approx)
Emanuel Steward and John Davimos	$119,279.25
Subtotal	$259,722.50
Plus:	
Purse and training expenses	$250,215.37
Final total	$509,937.87
Money received	$508,494.00
Shortfall	$1,443.87

In Warren's released statement, he said non-contractual payments totalled $258,277.63, so that would account for the rounding-up of the hotel bills and air fares and the minor discrepancy overall.

The McClellans do not have a problem with that. The devil in the detail is the payment due to Steward and Davimos. Lisa says she knew the money had to be paid to Gerald's former handlers, but maintains that Don King had agreed to make that payment – as the above accounts suggest he did.

This is where the argument switched to one between Davimos and King. In March of '96, the *Detroit News* spoke to both parties. Unsurprisingly, they gave conflicting versions of events.

Greg Logan reported:

Davimos said he and Steward went to court to recover that amount [$119,275.25] from McClellan because he had not paid them for his previous fights with them. 'Gerald told me Don

138

King was going to pay the $119,000,' Davimos said. 'Two days before the Benn fight, I got a check from Don King Productions for $119,000. Immediately after the fight, Don King stopped payment on the check. I said, "No chance. You made a deal with Gerald. I'll force the judgment." King said, "Gerald is in this situation; you can't take the money." I told Don I'd pick my own charities. Who knew he was going to take it out of Gerald's purse?'

The report added:

King agreed he asked Davimos and Steward not to take the money, saying, 'These two guys are so cold-blooded they didn't give [the McClellans] a dime.' But King denied Lisa's claim he promised to pay the $119,000 judgment.

King claims – and Lisa does not essentially dispute – that he has paid $169,557.69 he was not contractually obliged to, in helping with medical expenses after the fight. It's the Steward–Davimos settlement that she cavils at, as well as deductions for expenses that reduced Gerald's final cheque for the fight to $62,920.75.

Where did it all go? Into the abyss of professional boxing. Fighters who look at the upfront figures for a major, career-defining contest and imagine that is what they are going to end up with, are invariably disappointed. Their hardest fights come when the other guy stops hitting, when the lights go down and the lawyers come back in the room. There is probably a right and a wrong in there somewhere in this mess, and who could deny that for a renowned challenger such as McClellan to be left with such a skinny financial return in a fight that attracted such attention and created such interest was unfair? But boxing will never be about what is fair or right. It will always be about making the best that comes your way.

15

Freeport

Nearly five years after the fight the story had gone as quiet as Gerald. There had been the odd re-examination. *Sports Illustrated* went to Freeport a year after the fight to see McClellan. The Chicago paper visited. The mayor thought about naming a street after him. Didn't happen. Their best fighter had burned so brightly, now the lights had dimmed.

Gerald sits in the dark in his house at the bottom of Wyandotte Street, a cul-de-sac. Metaphorically and literally, he is going nowhere. He is oblivious to everything but the minutiae of his existence. The last clear images he saw, probably, were Stan and Donnie in the back of the ambulance.

I had to go and see him, even if he could not see me, or tell me anything about the fight or what happened either side of it. Those few who were allowed into his world said Gerald still had an amazingly strong spirit, that he had adjusted to his new, reduced life. To get to Gerald, though, I had to go through Lisa. She said to ring when I got there. She'd see. I'd come a long way but that did not mean the last mile was going to be easy.

Steward's Kronk gym web site has an address for donations for Gerald. There were a couple of such sites. I'd promised Lisa I'd make a contribution, but I wanted to be sure it was going to end up in the right place. I think it did.

Saturday afternoon, and the twin-prop plane from Detroit settles down on the empty concrete of Rockford Airport. The dozen passengers pile into waiting cars. I, however, had arrived in the four-wheel centre of the universe without a car, or even a driving licence. No sign of a cab.

I hump my bag the mile or so into town, find a bar, ask the proprietor if he can whistle up a driver of any description, and get a deranged Vietnam vet who charges me $50 to sit in the back seat of his filthy, probably lethal, vehicle, listening to tales of his daring against Charlie, not to mention the time he and his buddies beat up some London bobbies at Heathrow Airport when they 'were just messin' around on furlough'.

Freeport was forty miles south-east. All of a sudden, forty miles was a long way. Nice country, though. Brightly painted farmhouses plonked in the middle of safe, quiet fields. Uncomplicated bits of earth.

'Freeport?' says my guide to anarchy. 'Drive-by shootings, drugs – you name it, you got it in Freeport.'

Forty miles of what sounds like total horseshit later, Freeport looms.

'That motel, right there. That'll do . . . keep the change. Be lucky . . . Rambo.'

In the motel bar, Boring Bob serves customers with the annoying flippancy of the practised smart-arse: swings around to the optics without looking, all the while polishing glasses, rubbing down the counter, fiddling with the ashtrays, lecturing and telling lame gags, checking out the scores on the TV. Yankees and the Braves, first game of the World Series. Two guys from Rockford are drinking together, and we talk. Maybe Rockford was closed tonight. Long way to come to listen to Bob, though. Bob must have known more about every subject anyone mentioned than any barman in the history of barmen. He wasn't brilliant, however, on boxing.

'George McClellan, you say? . . . Oh yeah. Fighter, right? Oh. Gerald, you say? Yeah. Lives right here in Freeport. Got hurt, right? Never seen him, though. He win a world title or somethin'?'

Just serve, Bob.

Sunday mornings bring the quietest times in very quiet places.

For some people, they're the hung-over backside of Saturday. Sober types, who hadn't gone out, go to worship, or settle down and read the papers, look out on the world with a coffee and a firmly held opinion. This Sunday morning was its usual crisp, Boring-Bob self, autumn leaves falling about the streets, and, down on Wyandotte Street, Gerald was waking up on the first day of his thirty-fifth year.

Dented cars cruised peopleless streets around his neat house, where he'd always return after fights, even when he was having a good time in tougher, more interesting away-streets. Now, the world gets by without his input.

That morning, Freeport and America were as ordinary and quirky as on most other days. Guys on sunny corners talked about the Yankees beating the Braves 4–1 the night before, like Bob said they would.

The Governor of Illinois, a Republican, was in Havana being nice to the Cubans, according to the *Rockford Register Star*. On the TV, there were pictures from New York – the Klan were on the march, unmasked, and 8,000 people turned up to tell all sixteen of them to get back to Alabama, or wherever. A young boy from near Detroit, over in Michigan, was on trial for murder. The price of cigarettes went up thirteen cents. Pat Buchanan was leaving the Republican Party.

And, back home, Tottenham Hotspur had beaten Manchester United 3–1. Doubted the kids lurking on the corner cared much about that one. 'Hey! Cummere!' they shout as I take a walk to shake loose the shit in my head from the night before. I decline their invitation. They laugh that laugh without smiles.

Not far from where Gerald lives, there are an unusually large number of churches – so citizens do congregate there, in the most literal sense. Not much else. Just street after street of reasonably nice houses. And churches. There seems to be a certain righteousness running through the spine of the town. There are fifty-six churches, nearly all of them Protestant. In one half-mile stroll, I pass the First English Reformed (founded 1905), now called the Friendship Baptist; the First Lutheran; St Joseph's Catholic; Embury United Methodist; the Second Presbyterian; and the Holy Cross Greek Orthodox. That's enough religious diversity for one block.

Round the corner are the usual collection of small shops. Walt's Pawn and Music, Glick's Triangle Groceries – 'only one student at a time'. At the garage, a clipping from the local paper is pinned up in the window: 'Robber uses Lego gun to hold up gas station.' So much for the drive-by shootings.

This is how his friends and family prefer to remember Gerald McClellan, young and full of life. © *Vanessa Winship.*

Freeport, set up near the Pecatonica River in 1827 after the Winnebago Indians had been driven away, is averagely small-town Midwest. It used to be known as Pretzel City USA. They made pretzels here. To go with the beer the German settlers made. The other most famous thing about Freeport is it is the home town of Calista Flockhart – Ally McBeal. Robert Johns, who founded Black Entertainment TV, comes from here too.

Black folks always had to fight for what they had around Freeport. They were drafted in when the Italians who ran the railway went on strike. The blacks stayed. The Italians went off to New York.

The Mississippi is thirty-five miles to the west. There are about fifteen townships in this *Huckleberry Finn* setting, all still with strong German roots. In 1860, for instance, the year Heenan went to England to fight Sayers, there were 186 New Yorkers, 113 Germans and 30 Irish living in Freeport.

Now there are 25,000 Freeporters, 22,000 of them white, 3,000 black. In the nineteenth century, what blacks there were had been pretty much invisible in Freeport until the town got famous for a day: 27 August 1858.

That was when Abraham Lincoln came to town. Illinois Republicans had picked him to run against Stephen Douglas, whose view on slavery was that settlers should be allowed to decide for themselves if they wanted it or not. Abe and Steve debated the issue in Freeport in front of 20,000 people.

Theodore Roosevelt, commemorating the event with the dedication of a plaque in the town, described the debate as 'one of those memorable scenes in accordance with which the whole future of a nation is moulded'. You could say that. The result, a points win to Abe, lost Douglas sympathy in the South and split the Democratic Party. Lincoln went on to become president in 1860, precipitating the Civil War.

There's a statue on the site of the Lincoln–Douglas debate, of Abe and Steve, 'dedicated to the people of Freeport and their on-going efforts for racial harmony'.

Not sure how much of that Gerald saw growing up. Stan reckoned Gerald was not a big 'whitey lover', especially white women. Generally, he liked to move in his own circles. Still, this was not a town of seething prejudice, as far as I could make out.

Freeport's got all the ordinary stuff a small town usually has, all the activities that keep a community ticking over, all the modern fallibilities too. I saw ads and notices for six exercise classes, bridge and table tennis for pensioners, a 'Bosom Buddies Support Group for Women with breast cancer', a PTA meeting, Parents Anonymous, AA New Beginnings Women's Group, Cocaine Anonymous, nine other AA meetings in the district and one for Narcotics Anonymous.

There are six banks. Unemployment is 5 per cent. Ten per cent of the population are divorced. There are plenty of millionaires. It gets really cold in winter. This is a place of such profound insularity folks might boast about having a passport.

I've been in stranger places.

The corner house on South Carroll was neat and unpretentious. This was Lisa's house. I'd rung her from the motel to arrange to meet Gerald. She said we'd meet first at her place.

Candles on a makeshift altar in the corner of the front room (curtains drawn) lent an eerie presence and the huge dog outside let you know not to mess with the occupants. It was like a thousand other ordinary houses in Freeport, in a quiet and ordinary street, fenceless, grass clipped, fly-net door. Locked. Except it was different too. At various stages over the previous five years, this had been Chaos HQ.

I thought I was going to meet Lisa in Detroit, at the Hamed–Soto fight. But she didn't go. She watched it on TV, thought Naz was terrible. Wanted to see him 'get his ass kicked'. Not because Steward had been in Hamed's corner. Not because Manny used to train Gerald and split over money before Gerald fought Nigel. I got the impression, Lisa held no grudge against Manny. But she didn't like that little guy from England.

The McClellan family was consumed by drama on a Shakespearean level. Lisa was still rowing with everyone from King to the fighter's father about money. Her mother Genola, a heavy drinker, had died in a house fire. Don King told me in London three weeks earlier that he still sent Gerald money. Lisa supplied a different version. There are not many events in this saga that provoke universal agreement.

Meanwhile, general boxing news made little impact on Gerald. There was the debut of Muhammad Ali's daughter Laila, three weeks previously; the first man–woman fight that same weekend; *Newsweek*'s subsequent absurd story of an Ali comeback at fifty-eight . . .

He's better off not knowing all this.

So, how was Gerald's party?

'Oh yeah. It was real cute,' says Lisa. This was an encouragingly ordinary start to our conversation. Maybe getting to see Gerald was not going to be as hard as I'd thought.

'Everyone was coming up and wishin' him happy birthday and he said, "Today can't be my birthday," and I said, "Well, why not?" He said, "Well, how come I don't have any wine coolers?"'

Gerald had put on his best jewellery, including a $20,000 gold chain, a 'G' with diamonds on it and a Rolex ring, even though it was too tight and got stuck on his finger.

After a while, Gerald went to his bedroom to rest. A cousin went to see him and came back, worried. 'Did you take Gerald's jewellery off?' he asked.

'Gerald would never let anyone take it off him,' Lisa told her cousin. Sandra, the older sister, locked the doors. She was going to search everyone. Then Gerald pulled the chain out of his pocket. Nevertheless, the thought had occurred to the McClellans that somebody might have stolen a chain from a blind man at his own birthday party.

The sisters tried to put the rest of his jewellery in the safe. 'Get away from me!' he said. But he gave it to Lisa. She was the only one he'd let touch his jewellery. His life since the fight has been one of shifting trust. But you've got to trust somebody.

The ring, meanwhile, wouldn't budge from his finger. They called the doctor but Gerald wouldn't let him cut it off. He slept with his hand above his head instead, and his sister Stacey finally managed to twist it free during the night.

In a way, the fuss over the jewellery was a microcosm of his life, people haggling over bits of him. As hard as he'd tried, he'd never really had control of anything, except maybe his pit bulls.

There had been a lot of family there for his thirty-fourth birthday, including Emmite. This was one of those times when he and the sisters were talking, apparently.

Did they take any pictures?

'I was going to,' Lisa said, 'but my camera went missing twenty minutes into the party.'

We fell into easy talking. I wondered what life was like for this formidable woman. Everyone had a Lisa story. Not many of them ended happily ever after.

As Don King found out. She saw off some of his associates once, she said. She and Don had argued on the radio a few years back, sometime after the fight, over Gerald. Don was being interviewed and she rang up. They started shouting. She said he'd never looked after Gerald. He said he had. Don lost his cool, a rarity.

Her husband, Steve Jordan, moved pretty quickly about her skirt. Didn't say much. I heard later they'd split up. Clearly she was a woman not to be messed about. Still, we spoke with some amicability. She would let me see Gerald, but first we would talk.

Lisa said she'd cancelled a biography that a lawyer from California was writing about Gerald. 'Goddam, he only wanted to call it *Live by the Sword, Die by the Sword*. Well, Gerald ain't dead, right? So I called a stop to that one.'

The writer, Stephen Donovan, had organised the first fundraiser for Gerald in Freeport when he came home. A lot of fight people turned up for that one: Holyfield, Frazier, some locals even. Gerald stayed in another room. Lisa reckoned he didn't want the world to see him. You could understand that. But Donovan was trying to help. He'd written ten chapters, then finito. It didn't seem like he was the biggest villain of the piece.

Anyway, Lisa had 'a lotta horseshit' she wanted to straighten out before I could see her brother. It was obvious she loved Gerald, in a fierce and often confrontational way.

'Before,' she says, 'Gerald was . . . a piece of work! He was . . . very arrogant. Gerald and I are a lot alike, we're, like, eleven months apart and we are, like, so much alike.'

Nobody would argue with that. They're both pushy, outspoken. And, I would reckon, bullies. Lisa says she was one of the few people who would 'take him on'. Mostly, he got away with a lot.

'It didn't matter to me who he was and how much money he had. I treated him like I did my other five brothers and he didn't like that. We used to have fist fights. Oh yeah. Up until he got hurt.'

She took Gerald to task once when he was getting ready for a fight that never happened, against Terry Norris. Lisa told a friend of Gerald's he hadn't been training properly, that he should call the fight off. Steward had been looking for him, but Gerald was out with friends, on the street.

'So I'm at home,' she says, 'and my front door kicked open and it was him, and he said that I said he was gonna get beat or whatever and we actually had a physical confrontation. And I wasn't afraid of him and I always stood up to him.'

And now?

'Oh yeah, we still fight. Matter of fact, he chased me the other day. Even now I don't treat Gerald like he's handicapped, an invalid.'

A week or so before, she had to tell him off for pulling at the back of the sofa. He said he'd do what he wanted. It was his sofa, and she could get the hell out of his house. Lisa 'popped him on the hand', and he got out of his chair and chased her.

'If he woulda caught me . . . he probably woulda really hurt me.'

This is a comic and sad picture. Where once Gerald was a hard-core street guy, he is now a naughty boy, but one with a trained power and who still knows how to hurt. His sisters use a wheelchair to take him to the doctors, but otherwise he gets about with a frame. He will sit on his verandah, when it's warm. Or sometimes sit in his front room, curtains drawn, and play with his talking watch or listen to the television. He doesn't listen to TV so much, though. He likes to put pictures to the words, and that's not possible any more.

Three times a week they walk Gerald to the end of his block, then walk him back and put him on his treadmill. They try to get him to do floor exercises, but the ex-fighter doesn't see the point any more. 'I'm not doin' exercise,' he'll tell his sisters, 'I'm going to bed.'

Lisa, Sandra and Stacey used to look after Gerald in three eight-hour shifts every day. Last time I spoke to Lisa, Stacey had been dropped from the roster. But that was then. The McClellan clan are so volatile, Stacey might well be back in the fold.

'My sisters qualified as nurses, I didn't finish. Gerald don't like doctors, for some reason. We took him to the Mayo Clinic and he didn't even want the doctors to touch him. Which I thought was very strange. I dunno. I think that maybe in the back of his mind he was aware of something that somebody did to him.'

If this is a coded dig at the treatment he received in London, it is misguided. Gerald could not have had better care. There were stories, though, that while being transported between hospitals back in the United States, some instruments came free which might have had an adverse effect on his recovery. Lisa denies this.

There have been a few fund-raisers for Gerald, but Lisa thinks people have pretty much forgotten about her brother. She's right.

The boxing photographer Teddy Blackburn calls regularly. Teddy, who boxed a bit as an amateur around Ann Arbor, Michigan, hit it off with Gerald in Las Vegas years ago when they had an argument over a photograph. Gerald likes people to stand up to him, Lisa says.

Sometimes.

'Michael Moorer calls a lot. There's a guy who worked for Joe Frazier, but now he works for Emanuel, he calls a lot, a guy called Richard Slone. He did a painting of Gerald. My friend Pam bought it. Joe calls. Joe come to see him too. He lives in Philly. Ali sent a card the other day. Evander calls.'

Anyone else?

'If Stan came up he get his ass whupped. Donnie was here a coupla months ago. I'm OK with Donnie. I mean, Donnie's family.' She'd even made up with her father, who'd been at the party. One would hope they are still talking to each other.

You could only marvel at how the family could put up with the constant aggravation that has characterised their relationships since February of '95. But for some people, trouble and fighting are part of the fabric of their existence. In that, Lisa is more like Nigel Benn than she knows.

She stops to read bits of Nigel's autobiography, which I brought over for her.

'Hmmm,' she says, still reading. There is no softening of her attitude to Benn, whom she thought was insensitive towards her brother in statements he made after the fight. She has all the British newspaper cuttings.

About a year after the fight, Peter DeFreitas rang Lisa. He wanted to know if Nigel could come to see Gerald. He got a short answer. I wondered why.

'He asked what could they do to make us happy, what could Nigel do for Gerald. I can't even remember how long after it was . . . months. And, anyway, I made the comment: "Pay some of his fuckin' medical bills. You wanna do somethin' for him, pansy? Pay his medical bills!"'

She spits the words.

'And the reason that I have that attitude is because of all the things that I have read. You know? What's he gonna come here for? Why come here after he said, "I wish he die"? What you gonna come here for?'

At this point, I reckon my chances of seeing Gerald are diminishing in direct proportion to the rise in Lisa's vitriol.

'And I asked him, "Why you callin' and not Nigel?" You know? If I was in a car accident and I hurt someone I gonna follow through to be supportive of that person, to do what I can for that person, even if I don't have any money to give 'em. I still show my concern, from beginning to end. You know? I remember a reporter call me from Benn's last fight and said, "Nigel just lost, what do you have to say about it?" What am I supposed to say? He got beaten real bad, by Steve Collins. Good.'

Nigel was concerned to be seen as the sort of guy who would fight until he dropped and did not appreciate remarks by Naseem Hamed after he turned away from Collins in that last fight. Hamed said he would have fought until they chopped his arms and legs off. What did Lisa think of that?

'If I was in a situation like Nigel in his last fight and I couldn't continue, I'd stop. To hell with anybody else who had anything else to say about it . . .'

Would there be any circumstances under which the family would see Nigel?

'No.'

Would they take money if he offered it?

(Dumb question.)

'You damn right I would! You damn right! Because Gerald needs it! If he offered to make a donation to Gerald's trust fund, I'd be a fool not to take it! But I don't want to see his damn face!'

Lisa, who is more agitated now than earlier, continues to thumb Benn's book. She doesn't believe he said 'sorry' to Gerald in the hospital after the fight. There is no reason to disbelieve the story, but she won't have it.

'Maybe I'm not so trustin' in what people say.'

Her friend Pam interjects: 'I think maybe the family would have a bit more respect for him if he picked up the phone once in a while to see how Gerald was.'

'I spoke to Michael Watson's mother,' Lisa said, 'and they wrote a letter, it was a really nice letter, and they came to the hospital in London and they were very supportive of my family that was over there. But Nigel could have been just as well. You know? It was, like, Gerald is lying in hospital, and we didn't know if it was going to be life or death. At that time it was still a fifty-fifty chance he still coulda die, and the most important thing for Nigel is his interviews, you know? And he never called any of our family while they was over there. This stuff didn't happen until later. Where was he from the time Gerald got hurt until the time we started readin' all this stuff in the papers? So, you tell me! You tell me! Where was he all that time?'

There really wasn't an answer to that.

'I would never, ever, ever, ever say I wish [Nigel] was dead. Never, never. I may have said, "I wish him all the bad luck in the world." But I never would have wished him dead. Even if the media got this stuff all wrong and Nigel never said any of those things, he had a chance to make a difference and he didn't.'

What, I ventured, would Lisa have thought had Nigel been left disabled – and what would Gerald have thought?

'I think he would have been devastated. I think he would not have boxed, or I think he would not have been able to successfully box again.'

This tough, uncompromising woman suddenly seems profoundly sad. Our exchange has brought a lot of bad stuff to the top again. I reckon she hates Nigel, but wishes she didn't have to.

For his part, Nigel deals with it his own way. I asked him a couple of years ago if he would see Gerald. He didn't want to think about that. Later, after he'd found God, I asked him, through his agent Kevin Lueshing, if he'd changed his mind.

'Put it this way,' Lueshing said, 'Nigel knows his way around. He knows what would happen if he went there and maybe said just one thing that was taken the wrong way. The whole thing would kick off. It would be awful. I don't think that would be good for anyone.'

It would be the toughest thing Nigel could ever have done too. Tougher than any of his fights. Tougher than his fight with Gerald. He'd left it too long, that was obvious. To go back now, so many years later . . . that would take a serious amount of bottle. Maybe that's why he'd turned to God, to look for comfort outside his own environment, a world of little forgiveness.

The McClellans were passably religious, more so since the death of their mother around the Christmas of '98.

Gerald had embraced his religion, although he didn't attend services. He was brought up a Baptist and one night sat bolt upright – much as William Blake had done the night he died – and began singing an old gospel song from his youth.

'I had forgot it,' Lisa said, 'something we used to sing. Usually when I walk him to bed at night, I will sit on the bed and talk and we'll bring up a lot of old stuff from the past and, that's me and his time, at night. And I say, "You know I can't sing!" I sing to him, and I'll sing one part and he'll sing the other part, and if I sing somethin' wrong, he'll correct me and tell me that's not how to sing it.'

I ask her how bad a singer she is, and, for the only time during our meeting, she laughs, goes a bit shy. We stop for a second, like a rest between rounds. Then she reveals she made a video of Gerald a couple of years earlier and was going to send it to Nigel. She was going to send one to Don King too. 'But . . . I dunno. Never did. Seemed like a good idea at the time.'

She says the anger has disappeared, that it's like 'a bad memory gone wrong', which sounds doubly nihilistic. A bad memory. No good memories to go wrong.

They all try to think about the future. There are slivers of hope.

He's got three children: two sons, the eldest, Gerald Jr, who was living in Atlanta until Gerald brought him up to Freeport to live with her; Mandale, who lives in Detroit with his mother; and Forrest, his daughter, who lives in Freeport too. Three kids, three mothers. Gerald got about when he was young.

Now, though, he is a good father. The swirling mix of emotions that caused his youth to be played out in a quiet rage are distilled and redirected to those closest to him.

Gerald Jr, or Little G-Man as the family call him, slipped into his father's bedroom early one morning. Lisa eavesdropped on them.

'I don't think either one of them knew I was watchin', and Gerald was tellin' him, "Daddy really loves you, and you take care of your momma and go to school and you do good." And it was so touching. When his kids are around, he's like a take-charge kinda guy.'

Once he had Forrest over at the house, pulled her up on his knee and said, 'Come here and give Daddy a hug.' Over and over, he kept saying to her, 'Now Daddy loves his little girl, you know that? Now you tell me back that you love Daddy.'

She did. He loves to hear that. And he likes to play Dad, likes to know that his children are dressed well, have neat haircuts and their shoes polished. When he felt Little G-Man's Afro hairstyle once, he told him, 'You need a haircut, where's your mom? I whippin' your mom's ass, she should know better to let your hair grow like this.'

This is McClellan's world. His kids, his gadgets, his regime. He doesn't remember much outside of that world. He knew he was a fighter, a world champion. He remembers names now and again, but mixes them up. Mostly, his mind now is kept for quieter things. Like the birthdays of his sisters and children and other members of the extended family. He never forgets those, says Lisa.

'But he also remembers, like, what year he boxed in London for the first time. And when he fought Nigel. He remembers the two losses he had, the year the losses were in. He got those confused before. The last two fights before Nigel, he used to think they were the two that he lost.'

There was no medical possibility, was there, that Gerald would regain his sight?

'Maybe not, medically,' says Lisa. 'It ain't likely. But I think God has the last say. You know, I still believe that he's gonna get it back. Oh yeah. I do. I believe that he's gonna get it back. And I've had dreams that he's gonna get it back.'

We stop talking again.

'I wish Gerald had just said, "Hey, I'm through." I wish he would have . . .'

She looks like she might cry.

As I leave, I ask if I can see Gerald. Her face goes hard again.

'Ring me,' she says.

Unable to face Boring Bob in the bar again, I go to my room, a cell with no outside window. The local radio station, Star 92.1, is burbling away while I wait an appropriate time before calling Lisa. 'The tractor pull is at six thirty tonight at the county fair. Be there!'

I check out the tractor pull. A lot of country people eating hot dogs and drinking lemonade. Young guys spitting. Took me back to the agricultural shows of my youth. People walk by peering at large pumpkins. Everyone seems to know each other. Nearly all are white. I get the impression that to grow up black in Freeport you arranged an alternative life to go with the one laid on for you.

The Deputy Chief of Police, Robert Smith, tells me Freeport is an 'averagely criminal' sort of town. Shelley, who gave me a lift back to Rockford later, said, 'The cops keep the lid on a lot of trouble. It's there but you just don't see it.'

She'd had a little run-in in a bar one night with Lisa. Todd, who was carrying a gun, got involved and they had to call the police. Shelley said she'd send her kids to the Catholic school. Safer, she reckoned. Didn't want her kids – which she'd yet to produce – mixing with the wrong type. Freeport cannot be the only town in the world where parents cling to God for non-religious reasons.

Down the street from the police station, I pass the Salvation Army Community Center, 'T. David and Randi Bump, presiding. Soup kitchen, Monday to Friday.'

'Hello, Lisa? Yes, Kevin. OK . . . right. Well, I'll be in touch.'

I'd have to come back some other time, she said. It wasn't convenient right now.

Like I say, I've been in stranger places.

16

Of All the Bars . . .

So, I'd go home. Come back later. Maybe there would be a more convenient time to see Gerald. My flight went back through Chicago, and, as my stay in Freeport had been cut short, I had a night to kill.

With no time to go downtown, I booked in at a hotel near O'Hare Airport. One night's worth of diluted Chicago, listening to aeroplanes. It was an overpriced dump. I would tell you which one but the lawyer wouldn't allow it – like so much else in this story. Normally, you can move about America assured of at least a practised smile. This was a morgue. It stank of transient nothingness.

Nothing for it. Hit the bar – and pray Bob didn't have a cousin working in Rosemont.

A guy hoves into view. In a dinner jacket. He's either the resident comic – God, help me – or a boxing referee. Would you believe it? He's a boxing referee. I've booked into the one hotel in the whole of Chicago where that night there's boxing. It's $50 a ticket.

'Yeah, I'm on duty tonight,' he says. Friendly type. We fall to bullshitting each other. Turns out he's from Chicago and he used to be a trainer. Used to train in a downtown gym where the former European light-middleweight champion Jimmy Batten trained for a year.

'You remember Jimmy?'

Not many do. I only saw him box a couple of times. Interviewed him for the *Sunday Times*, about 1987. He worked around the corner from the office then, drove a minicab. He was angling for a payment, settled for a Chinese meal. Jimmy'd been good, but he'd been stitched up from time to time. He'd gone to America, like Steve Collins, like Kevin Sanders, looking to feed off the myth and legend that was the 'baahxin' bizness'.

He'd fought Roberto Duran in the States. 'Would have won if Terry Lawless had come over from London to be in my corner,' he said.

Towards the end, the British Boxing Board of Control called Jimmy in, thought he was punchy. 'They made me walk this thin line, to see if my balance was OK. Like they used to do with drunks down the nick. So, I lined it up and ran down it. Nothing they could do.'

There was. They took his licence off him. Jimmy was finished as a fighter. He took to making people laugh for a living. Had a go at *EastEnders*, as an extra in the Queen Vic. He fancied himself as a comic actor, rather than a comedian. But the breaks didn't come and he had to get up on the stage, eventually. 'It went OK.'

Next time I saw him, he had slash marks down his face. He'd been in a row in a club in the East End. This night, he was trying to gib his way into White Hart Lane to watch Frank Bruno fight Joe Bugner. I think he managed it.

'How 'bout that, eh? Jimmy Batten . . . Give him my best, OK?'

Never caught the ref's name. Next I saw him, he was up in the ring, waving his arms about in front of a boxer who was losing with considerable expertise. It was second fight on. The fighter looked very familiar. So did his trainer . . .

They've billed the main event as for the Illinois state title. Right. As if anyone'd notice.

'Ladeez and gentlemen!' comes the familiar bark from centre ring. 'Give it up for Mr Buzz Killman!'

Buzz murders the national anthem. It's one of those terrific American institutions. Everyone does it. Before the Super Bowl. Fights. Everywhere. They get up and they slaughter the song they hold most sacred. And people say they've got no sense of humour.

Buzz is doing just fine in the aural homicide stakes. Somehow he gets through it. 'Jeez,' he says, 'I guess I'm going to have practise that one and get back to y'all.'

A guy called Tyrone Handy is first up. After a couple of seconds it's plain his fighting name should be 'Not So'. Buzz had encouraged the patrons to 'give it up' for the girls from Budweiser, who would be carrying the round cards. Tyrone doesn't make it to the first Bud. He gets sparked in one, by someone called Carlos. It lasts two minutes and twenty seconds.

Carlos and Tyrone missed out on Jennifer. She's the first Bud bird. Jenny is a brave girl. I've not seen a round-card girl before whose cellulite takes up more space than her breasts. She's standing there, anyhow, as the next two get in.

I go to the bar. When I come back, there's my new referee friend waving his arms about. And damn, if the trainer with the sailor's hat isn't my old pal Stan.

Under his tutelage this evening was a pugilist by the name of 'Vicious' Christian, 'fighting out of Milwaukee in the wonderful state of Wisconsin!'

Vicious was up against a Puerto Rican called Danny Paez, two fights, two wins. For three minutes they conspired to miss each other with every punch they threw. These guys missed targets like America missed the starts of world wars.

Vicious had an excuse. He was a foot shorter than Dan, with arms like saveloys. Dan just couldn't box. If they ever find the two guys he beat, they should gently lead them away. If you can't box, you can't box. Danny Paez can't box. He wins.

Buzz is buzzing. 'Guys,' he says, talking to me and a couple of hundred assorted desperates with nothing better to do on a Wednesday night, 'who wouldn't want the shirt that Jade is wearing, eh! Yeah! Me too!'

Jade slings some shirts into the bog of humanity of which I am a part. She is joined by Cellulite Jenny and Yvette, who is a looker. They throw all kinds of trinkets at us, like feeding the pigeons. A small boy in front of me, wearing a Muslim skullcap, eases forward to catch a prize from the girls. Buzz is urging everyone to scream louder, and they do. The kid catches a T-shirt. Buzz is elated at the mob's response. 'Are you kidding me!' he shouts. 'This is professional boxing!'

But not as we know it, Buzz.

And then, next bout, Stan's back. They've got him on a conveyor belt, wheeling in one opponent after the other. Buzz gets the mike and tells us who the next victim will be. 'Outta Milwaukee, in the wonderful state of Wisconsin, give it up for the Black Battle Cat, ladeez and gentlemen! Mr Donnie Pendleton!'

Close. Penelton. Gerald's cousin. Still punching, after all these years. He's in against a local guy called James 'the Flame' Pointer. We 'give it up' for the Flame. He's 10–0. He weighs 161lb. Donnie weighs 169lb, and is announced as having had twenty-four professional fights. Like, when? In the past month? Donnie passed the twenty-four-fight mark a decade ago.

The Flame gets a workout and a W. Donnie gets maybe $1,500 and an L. But he boxes just fine. He's better than the Flame, I'll tell you that. But he's not here to inconvenience the kid. Pointer will move on. Donnie will just move out of the way. He gets the trip, though, and is unhurt. That's a result. That, in fact, amounts to a win for the Black Battle Cat.

Donnie's professional record was awesome in its awfulness. Born in Milwaukee, in 1964, he'd been fighting since 1990. In a decade of staggering underachievement, Donnie had fitted in 113 fights, winning nine (three by stoppage) and losing 102. It is a monument to optimism – or, in Donnie's case, realism and resignation. He has skill, but he discovered long ago he was not meant to be a winner. And a lot of people were happy that Donnie Penelton was a convincing loser.

I'm getting slowly drunk on bad wine. There are more T-shirts. More Buzz. More cellulite. And then Stan's back with another one. A girl. And she wins! Knocks her opponent out in one round.

Some local fighter gets in, loses and slopes off. I think this was the main event. Later, the guy comes back after what I assumed was the last bout, climbs in the ring again and makes a meal of saying goodbye to boxing. 'I can't do it no more,' he says, betraying no sense of the absurd. 'My body says no. I lost to a so-called fighter tonight, to this clown. But I'm here to say I feel with you. I'm going to miss you as much as you will miss me.'

Priceless. Then he thanks the promoter, a guy called Bobby Hitz, whom Stan fought a million years ago. 'I'm going into partnership with Bobby,' the breathless retiree tells a dozing and departing audience, 'so you haven't seen the last of Fearless!'

Some name. Some guy.

But wait! There's another fight! Stan's back with another body. It's Maurice 'Midnight' Virgil. Midnight's not bad. He weighs 165lb and, yes, he's from 'Milwaukee! In the wonderful state of Wisconsin!' The other guy, Oscar Somethingorother, weighs a couple of pounds more and has a 6–1 log with three KOs. Midnight will not be expected to win this one. He doesn't.

A little later . . .

We're in the bar. Stan, Donnie, Midnight, Vicious and a couple of others are gathered around my wallet. I think the girl who won was there too. I tell the guys I'm seeing Gerald. I'm going beyond drunk. So are they. But I've had a pretty good start. Even though they're drinking Martinis (three olives) and I'm on some plonk pretending to be Chardonnay. I wasn't so much nursing my drink as driving it at high speed to intensive care. It slips past twelve. We swap a lot of stories. I'm feeling pretty good.

Stan had said when we spoke on the phone that Donnie would ask me for money to talk about Gerald. The old Black Battle Cat certainly dropped hints when we spoke earlier. But now he's fine. We're at the bar. Face to face, and we're indulging in some top-of-the-range, late-night bollocks.

'I want to do something for Gerald,' Donnie says. 'I be going down there a lot. I took Stanley down there one time, coz the family so mad at him, so against him. It was like five years before he could see him, after the fight in London, England. They took a lot of stuff from us too. Took everything from us, practically took our livelihood from us when they did that to us. It was very difficult. The family got into it, tearing each other apart about it and stuff. That was sad.'

There are a couple of versions of what happened when Stan and Donnie came back from London in '95. What Lisa, Stan and Donnie agree on is that Don King told Gerald's seconds to go home and 'keep your motherfuckin' mouth shut'.

Stan, meanwhile, went back to Milwaukee and decided to talk. He called a press conference and brought along a selection of items from the fight.

'Everybody shows,' Stan remembers. 'Lisa shows too. And she

snatches some of the articles out of my hand. I had stuff I was gonna show people at the press conference. Nigel Benn hitting Gerald behind the head, I was showin' them a piece o' paper from the hospital where they'd made a cut in his head, stuff like that. And I was just going to explain to everyone there how Gerald was getting these wicked-ass punches at the back of his head, with all this tape on his glove. She snatched the newspaper from me and she said, "You ain't givin' no press conference on my brother." And I said, "This ain't about your brother, this is about me, motherfucker. I was there. Get the fuck outta here." '

We're not talking *Newsnight*.

'She's nothin'. She's a fuckin' louse. Gerald McClellan never liked that insolent sister of his. He always thought she a goofball. Why you never see her at no fight? Coz he wouldn't allow the bitch at the fight. She running around bossin', man, coz she run around bossin' her sisters all the time anyway. Coz she's a bully. Now she's in charge of everythin' and she shouldn't be in charge of shit. Never let me see Gerald.'

Lisa, naturally, would later dispute Stan's story. She said Donnie tipped her off that Johnson was selling Gerald's boxing kit at the press conference. She said she showed up to put a stop to that.

In the bar at the Rosemont, we're on about our third or fourth round of Martinis and Chardonnay. Stan's visit to Freeport, on the fifth anniversary of the fight, a Sunday morning, was his first since the fight. 'Snuck by and saw him. He knows me, he remembers me, he loves me, I still love him, man. He's a great guy. That happened to him and it bothered me, but, after seein' Gerald I been able to let go, you know what I mean? I don't blame myself.'

We'd been down this road, over the phone. But Stan, face to face, was angry. While he could have let it lie, after all these years, he wants justification. Some sort of moral closure. There was general agreement in our drinking circle that Gerald would not have let Stan stop the fight. Donnie and Stan were locked in a mutual pact of tragedy. Donnie was getting angry too.

'They robbed Gerald and I figured they robbed me and Stan. They robbed us of the championship ring! They took everything from us! They did nothin' for us! We came a long way with the kid,

Stan Johnson, rarely without his sailor's hat, was with Gerald at both ends of his career – but there was never any doubt who was in charge. © Vanessa Winship.

to get him there. Man, I was there with him from the beginnin'. Everybody wanna have a champion . . . But, hey, man, they took everythin' we damn well had . . .' He trailed off. 'You look at the fight, Gerald McClellan shoulda been the WBC super-middleweight champion of the world, man . . .'

We – I – get another round in.

'Everybody feel sorry for a great champion like Gerald. You know, you see him one minute, young kid, great champion, he got everythin' goin' for hisself. Now his life . . . he's just like a dead person sittin' there. All he can do is eat, y'know? That's like a bad feelin' there, man. Every time I go down there, I feel real bad. Cryin'.'

When they'd snuck up to Freeport to see Gerald, they'd all sat round crying. They all agreed Gerald was a hard and violent individual, but with a soft side.

'I think he was really a soft sonofabitch at heart,' Stan started in. 'I think that's what I saw with Deuce, first time I've ever seen any companionship in the guy. It was almost like maybe I was supposed to stop the fight in London, England, coz he stopped the fight with Deuce.'

A certain amount of repetition sets in. Not all of it from me.

What, I wanted to know, happened to Hyacinthus Turnipseed?

'We never seen him before. He was an old frienda Gerald's from Erie, Pennsylvania. You know, we walk in the Peacock gym. This kid there. Gerald said, man, I know that guy. Go all the way back to school there, with this kid . . . He left Freeport for a while, went back to Erie . . . This kid just pops up outta nowhere, you know? I didn't know him at all. When he popped up, everything got real strange.'

Donnie is now talking freely, and for free. He wasn't sure about Mr Turnipseed, for a start.

'I felt a lot strange about him. From Erie, Pennsylvania, then there he is. I didn't like that he was there, but I couldn't say anythin', coz Gerald was the champ, y'know?'

It was a crowded corner.

Nobody knows where Mr Turnipseed is. Believe me, I looked.

17

Meeting Gerald

Gerald's side of Freeport is handsomely run-down. Wooden bungalows, unfenced drives, torn fly-net doors, the odd flag, backyards with rumbling dogs, kids on the corner. On the face of it, neither heaven nor hell.

This night, I will finally get to meet Gerald in his neat bungalow at the bottom of Wyandotte Street. If anyone from outside gets to meet Gerald – and not many do – it's 90 per cent likely it will be in his house. He doesn't leave home a lot.

Lisa was going to take him on holidays a couple of years ago, up in the hills, to a cabin with Steve and a few friends and family. 'Wouldna been fair on the others,' she concluded. 'Gerald can be real demanding. He requires a lot of attention.'

She relishes the burden, it seems. I say to Steve, her husband, that it must be hard on everyone. He doesn't reply. He's used to it, I guess. Lisa has made her brother the centre of her life, it's her lot. She might think she deserves it, or she might think there will be a reward at the end, spiritual or temporal. Maybe both.

Lisa was quick to assure me that Gerald had improved significantly in his general health, although they are all still worried about his reluctance to go back to the Mayo Clinic to explore the slim chances of restoring his sight.

Teddy Blackburn, the boxing photographer, who has kept in touch with Gerald when others have dropped off, says it's not an easy visit to Wyandotte. Donnie said that too. It makes him cry. A lot of people Gerald knew as friends, who worked with him, made money with him, who admired him as a fighter, have not been to Wyandotte.

The person who finds it toughest is Todd McClellan.

For a long time, Todd, who has a place in Freeport, couldn't go to see his brother. In the end, it got to him. One day about four years ago, he took a tape of Gerald's last fight, walked outside to his driveway and smashed the bad memories to smithereens.

Todd was always the wild McClellan. He was the one who chose to walk away from boxing, to go with the gangs. In prison, he found the Disciples, a collective of like-minded citizens. Outside, he carried a gun. As had Gerald. But in the summer of 2000, Todd was out and intent on going straight.

Todd, who'd won sixty-nine of seventy-one amateur bouts, an impressive sixty-seven by stoppage, went down to a gym in Freeport, just off Main Street, and decided he was getting back into shape. At thirty-four, he was going to make a comeback.

It was the talk of the town for a few days. On 4 June 2000, the *Freeport Journal-Standard* led their front page with a story headlined, 'A brother's burden'. Todd had trained hard, it was reported, and was scheduled to make his return three weeks later at the local Masonic Temple 'against an opponent yet to be determined'. He would start slowly, he said, building up to the fight that had come to obsess him: A McClellan rematch against Nigel Benn.

'It would mean a lot to me and to my family for me to get a chance to knock him out,' he said. 'A majority [of my motivation] is revenge.'

Todd told the paper he hadn't fought in ten years – although Lisa and others said Todd had given up boxing as a teenager, just as he was scheduled to box Gerald in the Golden Gloves. Maybe he'd fought elsewhere. But the call of the street is what really did for Todd. As his sister said, 'He was a follower.'

He had been building up to this comeback for months; Lisa said in February that Todd was going to go to the Kronk to train with Manny Steward. He did not quite get the journey.

His trainer wouldn't be Hall-of-Famer Steward, but St Louis's Jim Howell, not previously a big name. Jim reckoned Todd had what it took.

His promoter wouldn't be the fight game's biggest mover, Don King, but one Doug Amundson, an old hand who enthused that Todd had 'the greatest motivation I've ever seen . . . Nothing's going to stop him.'

Todd says he was inspired to come back after reading Benn's

autobiography, *The Dark Destroyer*. I'd given a copy to Lisa, so I felt vaguely responsible for this, but Todd's a grown man. Very grown. He was outraged by what he reckoned Benn was saying in the book: 'They brought him over here to bash me up. Look at him now.' That was a liberal interpretation of Benn's view. There is contrition in his printed words; not an excess of it – but it's there. Like the feud between Ali and Frazier, that between McClellan and Benn was a lingering argument conducted over poor lines of communication distorted by time, distance and pride.

Todd had warmed up with a Toughman contest at nearby Rockford. The date was 25 February, the anniversary of Gerald's last fight. It was also the day that Donnie brought Stan and the boys to Gerald's house on Wyandotte to see his blind cousin. Lisa was out – which was just as well for Stan. Meanwhile, at the fights, Todd won five out of six bouts at heavyweight, and he figured that was a good sign.

Lisa knew, though, that Todd would never fight Benn. She knew her brother was dreaming. He hadn't told Gerald about his plan at that point. Gerald was a little confused, he said. He would tell him later.

The comeback might have been viable, but a revenge fight with Benn was a preposterous idea. Benn has a shadow on his brain and cannot go near a ring again. And Todd had his own problems, chief among them being a loose grip on reality. Only in the movies would such a revenge fight happen.

If Todd were to think more calmly about the possibilities on offer, a more profitable – although still wildly fanciful – goal might have been a fight against Gerald's old friend, Roy Jones Jr. Not only was Jones still active, but he had shown an implacable tendency to avoid dangerous opponents. Todd would not represent a serious threat – and it would provide a pay day for the McClellans. Gerald's funds were running precariously low.

There were several obvious problems.

Jones, the world's best in any weight category at or around twelve stone, the best pound-for-pound boxer in the world by most experts' reckoning, had been deeply upset by Gerald's plight. He had always admired McClellan, ever since their memorable contest as amateurs in 1988. Jones had lost, and both had suffered. A contemporary, John 'Iceman' Scully, said he saw Gerald a month later and the winner's ribs were still aching.

Jones has been quoted many times as saying he could not bear to visit Gerald until he retired. But Steward told me on a visit to London that Jones revealed to him he had, in fact, been to see McClellan. He had gone to Freeport quietly, spent some time with him on his own and then left. Jones won't talk about it while he's still boxing. 'Gerald's condition had a very, very deep effect on Roy,' Steward said. 'And that is why he will never be the fighter he could be. He always holds back. He doesn't want to risk ending up like Gerald. Simple as that. People think Roy is a hard man, but he's very sensitive, does a lot of work in the community, looks after boxers on undercards, makes sure they get paid well, things like that. Seeing Gerald really affected him.'

Steward, for the record, thinks McClellan at his best would have beaten Jones. Todd, though, was never as clever a boxer as Gerald. Now he was a memory of his old self – any serious boxer who loses even once in a Toughman contest has to question his credentials – and would have been embarrassingly outclassed. Still, in a sport where absurdity has never stood in the way of making money, stranger matches have been made.

The last I heard, though, Todd was back in prison. There would be no comeback ...

Gerald's house is the last one on the right. That's where the street ends. Near the old trainless railway line. It is an ordinary place, and anything but ordinary at the same time. Here is where Gerald sits as the noise swirls around him. The battle is all but done now, though. Lisa does not expect the fight to carry on. King has done his thing, she's hung in there, and they will all make the best of it. She, too, had contemplated a ring career. But she didn't think she could give up smoking to get in shape. When Gerald's money runs out, Lisa says she will move Gerald into her place. Stan reckons she will 'stick Gerry in a home'.

Lisa answers the door and I've yet to winkle a smile out of her. Steve busies himself around her, and goes into the kitchen to get tea ready. As I step inside, there on his green recliner is Gerald. This, as Blackburn had warned me, is a seriously disturbing moment.

In a way, any embarrassment or nervousness on a stranger's part is misplaced, given that McClellan would be unaware of who the stranger was, and not concerned anyway if the visitor was uneasy. Yet there was an undeniable feeling coming off the big man that he knew more about you than you imagined. Maybe it was a fighter's sixth sense.

Lisa introduces us.

'This is Kevin!' she shouts into McClellan's left ear, the one that works best. 'Kevin, Gerald! From London, England!'

There is no response.

'He's a writer! He's come from London, England, to say hello to you, Gerald! Say hello to Kevin!'

'Kevin?'

'Yes! From London, England!'

'London? London, England? Kevin? Kevin from London? London, England?'

Gerald asks Lisa what's the difference between a writer and a reporter. Reporters he'd met. They were the guys who took down what he said after he'd won a fight. Lisa tells her brother reporters work for newspapers; writers, well, they write other stuff, like books.

'How much you weigh, Kevin?'

'About twelve stone, Gerald.'

'Twelve stone? Twelve stone?'

That was McClellan's division when he finished up, super-middleweight. It's struck a chord. Except he never reached twelve stone. He levelled out three pounds under the limit for Benn. Nobody would ever know if that was a factor in his collapse in the later rounds. Steward suspected it was. So did Kevin Sanders.

I am sitting awkwardly on the edge of the couch next to Gerald. Lisa tells me to take hold of his hand and to squeeze it as hard as I can. I'm not in the best position to do this comfortably, but I grab Gerald's right hand, the hand that only a few years ago was one of the most feared in boxing, the one that had made McClellan briefly famous, the right he'd busted on Julian Jackson's head then, nearly a year later, had used to hammer Benn. The hand Sanders had watched Gerald wrap himself.

As our skins touch, Gerald's face comes to life. He bears down tight on my much smaller hand, crushing the knuckles into a ragged line. I am unable to do anything about it and will remain in this bizarre position, perched on the couch with my hand in the grip of a blind man, for at least another hour. We try to talk, but there is not much of what you could call dialogue. Still, Gerald makes an effort to engage. There is a warmth in his faltering voice. He'd like to know about this strange man who's landed up in his front room.

'Kevin? From London, England? Hey, Kevin. Why did you come? Why you come to see the G-Man?'

'To see how you are, Gerald. To say hello and to see how you are. To wish you well.'

I would learn that Gerald could not take in a sentence of that length all at once. His powers of comprehension have been so shredded, he can only communicate in bursts of a few words, repeated over and over, shouted into his ear, as you prick some sensation in him by squeezing his right hand or pinching him above the right shoulder. These are the magic zones of life in McClellan's wrecked body. I am overcome with admiration for his courage.

We continue to shout each other's names at each other for several minutes, as Lisa sits nearby, attending to her stricken brother in a schoolmarm way, chiding him here and there, all the time rubbing his shoulder. Her face is emotionless. She has been through this wringer for more than five years. There is nothing left to cry about. Or to smile about. I think I see why she is so hard.

Gerald wants to know why I'm staying in a hotel and not with him. Given that it has taken me two visits just to get inside his front door, I can't rationalise this easily, especially under these conditions.

'It was just easier, Gerald. Didn't want to intrude.'

'Intrude?'

It was not a word he might have used often. In his reduced state, Gerald can only trawl those words, gestures and memories that are most familiar to him. He doesn't know me, so there is nothing in his memory bank marked 'Kevin from London, England' to draw on. Our meeting is a fresh experience for him.

Most of the time his world is a repeat of all that has gone before, yesterday, last week, last year, his childhood. Sometimes, even, his boxing career. He knows he was a boxer. He knows he was hurt in London, England. But I can't begin to bring myself to mention the fight. I'm thinking of my own embarrassment, perhaps. But what could I possibly say to McClellan about it? Nice fight, Gerald. Shame about the result.

At this point we have a visitor. Little Gerald, McClellan's oldest son. He'd moved up from Atlanta that summer to live in Freeport with Lisa. He spends a lot of time at Wyandotte with his father. He looks at me much as Gerald must have looked at Stan Johnson all those years ago in Milwaukee.

We say hello. Or at least I do. He responds like all shy young twelve-year-olds. Mutely, with half a nod. He's just been to try out for the junior high school football team. It's the second try-out. Lisa tells him to put his football gear in the washing machine and he looks at her as if she's just asked him to fly to Mars.

'Nah. Can't do that.'

'Gerald, do as I say. They're dirty.'

Steve intervenes. 'Lisa, leave him alone. Don't you know you can't wash your football stuff until after the third try-out? It would look bad. You got to get them real dirty first, show the coach you're trying your hardest.'

'I don't care about that. Gerald, put 'em in the machine.'

'Nah. Can't do that.'

Gerald's father has been picking up bits of this domestic spat. He says something inaudible. Young Gerald goes over to his father, takes his hand and sits on the edge of his recliner. I am still propped up on the edge of the couch, with my right hand stuck in Gerald's.

'Hey, little G-Man! You make the team?'

Young Gerald is still not used to my presence. He strokes his father's hand and indicates that he'd rather not talk now, not in front of this guy, whoever he is.

'You do OK?'

'Yeah.'

Lisa gives Little G-Man some milk and biscuits and ushers him into the kitchen.

'Gerald!' she shouts in his ear. 'You want a cookie?'

He does. He always does. Gerald has got a sweet tooth, which is evident by his slightly ballooning frame. He's not grossly over-weight, maybe a couple of stone. But his exercise is minimal, despite the best efforts of his sisters to get him on his treadmill.

'Lisa! Lisa! You have a cookie too!'

Lisa pretends to eat her biscuit.

'Hey! You not eatin'!'

'How you know that Gerald?'

'Coz I got an eye in my ear!'

He laughs, weakly. In the circumstances of his predicament, it is a laugh that has the power of a thousand laughs. It is weirdly uplift-ing, a sliver of warmth in his life. Just a laugh.

The television is on in the background, with the sound down. When Gerald talks it is with a crackling energy that drowns out the TV. He is a reduced presence the rest of the time, much like Ali, whose Parkinson's syndrome subdues a once overpoweringly alive human being. Gerald was a notorious 'rounder', to use the American expression. He once could not sit still. Now he has no choice. His movement is restricted to mundane bodily tasks. It is a world of milk and cookies, of trips to the bathroom, of going to bed, of getting up. He embroiders the boredom with love. If his children and other family come close, Gerald pours emotion on them, and asks them to give some back. It is as if all those wild nights in Detroit, with Deuce and Stan and Donnie and a cast of other unknowns, was leading to this. He was no saint, but he was an average sinner, by all accounts. He has come home.

My hand has seized up. It really has. I can feel nothing in my fin-gers. There is a patch of my back that has gone numb too. The only sensation there is a dull ache. It's going to take a Scotch or two to get rid of that. It's enough to have been allowed briefly into his heart, a stranger indulged and welcomed, but the exercise in stuttering communication is painful. I feel like a voyeur. Little Gerald hovers, still looking silently. As I told Gerald, I don't want to intrude.

'I have to go now, Gerald!' I shout into his ear.

'Kevin? From London, England?'

'Yes! Thank you very much for having me in your house!'

'Hey, Kevin! Kevin! You stay with the G-Man next time, yeah?'

'Yes, Gerald! I'd like that. I'd like that very much!'

I prise my hand free. It is as white as a china plate. My back is in spasm. I stand up, physically drained and spiritually high. Gerald is led into his bedroom. His legs, which once conveyed him so smoothly around the ring, shift cumbersomely on their familiar journey. As he leaves the room, a horrible, cold emptiness takes his place.

I say goodbye to Lisa. She reminds me that Ben Bacon, of the *Sun*, had visited some years ago and promised to send her a chocolate bar, a brand he had with him but which wasn't sold in the US. 'He said he'd send some. You remind him.' I imagine I see a quarter of a smile on her sad face.

I thank Lisa for her time. And Little G-Man. He looks at the floor. Steve gives me a lift back to my hotel.

On the way back, Steve doesn't say much of anything either. As we near the hotel, we pass the gym where Todd had gone to get ready for his comeback. The thought occurred that his doomed hope of gaining revenge for his brother had an undeniable nobility about it.

If Todd was dreaming, he was only guilty of the same delusion that afflicts every boxer. It was a dream different only in its scope from the one he and Gerald had shared when sparring under the street lights of Freeport as kids.

Epilogue

Boxing is a natural home for dreamers. I've seen two of them die in pursuit of their reduced version of the big prize. Their names will mean little to many people today. They died a long time ago, a long way away. They were Roko Spanga, an Australian who boxed with willing competence at and around ten stone, and Chuck Wilburn, an American whose ambition was long behind him. They were both honest, brave men, never quite as good as they believed themselves to be, and who each had one hard fight too many. Their last contests were against the same man, Hector Thompson, a world-class lightweight and light-welterweight from Newcastle, New South Wales, near where I grew up.

Hector was a decent man, quietly spoken. Working on a local newspaper, I met him when he turned professional and he impressed me as a dedicated athlete with the right attitude to his sport. He knew the dangers and was prepared to take the risks because he dreamt of becoming a world champion. Maybe that's one reason it never occurred to me to question how he could carry on boxing after Spanga's death, in Newcastle in 1970. Or that of Wilburn in Sydney six years later.

From a distance, reporter and boxer seem callous. I can only claim callow wonderment. Boxing to me was still an untouchable mystery. Thompson, meanwhile, was entitled to keep his dream alive. Besides, he was almost as much a victim of the tragedies that touched his life as were the two men who died. He lived, but a part of him died too. It could have been him. If he knew that beforehand, why should it be any less true afterwards? Why should we adjust our morality in retrospect? If you go to the fight with a free heart and leave with a heavy one, it seems an act of intellectual skullduggery to pretend that was not always a possibility.

As Lisa reminded me, Gerald didn't die. Yet, but for quick

173

medical attention, he might have done – and I saw for myself that substantial parts of him have closed down. Some of Nigel died too, of course. While Benn still has his health, only he knows how much of his spirit is irretrievably gone. I suspect his turning to God a few years later represented a call for help, a way to retrieve something he lost the night he fought McClellan.

They all suffered enormously for our pleasure.

Why? Why do men allow themselves to be led to a ring and fight each other for nothing more tangible than glory or money – when the price can be death or a lifetime of half-death?

It is Pride. Ego. The need to establish an identity. To make a living the only (or most efficient) way some men know how. All of these. And something else, surely.

An American scientist, Dr Craig Venter, disturbed some unshakeable verities earlier this year when he concluded that man is not genetically superior to the rest of nature. 'In many cases,' he said, 'we have found that humans have nearly exactly the same [number of] genes as rats, mice, cats, dogs and even fruit flies.'

Of mice and men and fruit flies. All God's dumb creatures.

If we are biologically little better than animals, maybe it is our baseness that makes us fight, a deep, rarely tapped urge to survive that can never be wholly 'civilised'.

This drags the conclusions closer to Darwin and his idea of survival of the fittest than it does to Nietzsche, who saw something more cerebral in the struggle, who urged us to conquer our inner self, without God, to become Superman. The triumph of the will.

For me, Eddie Futch expressed it best. I asked the wonderful old trainer once why he thought boxing existed in a society that might know better. 'Men just fight,' was his simple response. 'Look at kids. They run about, compete against each other without thinking. It is just natural, it's in them.'

And Eddie knew the flip side to fighting. Eddie was the man who probably saved Joe Frazier's life.

When Eddie accompanied Joe to Manila for the third fight between Frazier and Muhammad Ali in 1975, the air stank with cheap language. Ali, at his worst, called Joe a gorilla. 'Ignorant.

Stupid. Ugly.' It slipped beyond pantomime. When Frazier heard what Ali said, he told Eddie, 'Whatever you do, whatever happens, don't stop the fight . . . I'm gonna eat this half-breed's heart right out of his chest. I mean it. This is the end of him or me.'

After fourteen rounds, Joe's right eye, his good one, was a purple mess and he could barely see. His body was closing down. So was Ali's. Futch, who knew Frazier's wife and children as friends, looked at him sitting spent on the stool and would not let Joe risk another three minutes. The most relieved man in the drama was not Joe, who felt cheated, but Ali. Joe and Eddie didn't find out until later, but Ali had had enough. He had 'gone through the trap-door', as he described it afterwards. Joe, however, was ready to risk suicide – which is why he harbours bitterness towards Ali to this day. Joe is even sore, still, at Eddie.

Certainly, he resents the insults levelled at him, arguing with some strength that Ali demeaned his fighting integrity, as well as his dignity as a man. That, in Joe's view, demanded retribution. But they'd fight each other no more – which opened up a bigger hurt for Joe. He reckons now that, if he'd come out for the fifteenth round, Ali would not have been there to meet him. There is good evidence for that view. People in Ali's corner alerted his trainer, Angelo Dundee, to what was happening on the other side of the ring, as Futch was motioning the referee over to tell him Joe was quitting. A second or two later, and it might have been Dundee telling the referee that Ali wanted to quit. And Frazier would have won what the fine American boxing writer Jerry Izenberg called 'the championship of each other' by two fights to one.

For Futch at that point, however, the result of a boxing match was irrelevant. In pulling Frazier out while there was even a trace of fight left in him, he made a decision not based on animal urges, thirst for revenge or smart philosophy. He was not driven by the macho leanings of unbruised Fight Writers or the considerations of those who had promoted the fight. Futch just knew that, however compromised, man always has a choice.

Like the mob descending on Sayers and Heenan, Eddie had saved Joe having to make that choice. So Joe could always say it wasn't him who quit. Frazier didn't like to quit altogether, though.

In his next bout, he even fought with contact lenses in. He boxed on too long for his own good, of course. Like Ali did, like Benn, like a thousand others. Futch only doused the fire for a moment. It flickered dangerously in Frazier's heart until even he could rise no more.

Joe is still one of the few fighters who makes the trip to the house at the bottom of Wyandotte Street. Sitting opposite him in the green recliner, he sees what might have been. And he knows Gerald is no motherfuckin' dog.

McClellan, at his home in Freeport, Illinois, manages a smile as he exhibits the World Boxing Council Middleweight belt he won when he knocked out Julian Jackson. © Teddy Blackburn.

The Fighters' Records

GERALD McCLELLAN

Born: Freeport, Illinois, 23 October 1967.
Height: 6ft.
Last registered fighting weight: 11st 11lb.

Amateur record
1984–1987: Wisconsin Golden Gloves champion.
1988: Runner-up, National Golden Gloves – beat Roy Jones, pts, semi-final; lost to Ray McElroy, pts, final.

Professional record
31 wins (29 stoppages), 3 losses (1 stoppage).
1991–1993: World Boxing Organisation middleweight champion.
1993–1994: World Boxing Council middleweight champion.

Estimated career earnings: $1 million.

1988
12 August: (Milwaukee), Roy Huntley	Win KO 1
15 September: (Glen Burnie), Bill Davis	W RSC 1
22 November: (Las Vegas), Ezequiel Obando	W RSC 1
25 November: (Auburn Hills), John Gordon	W RSC 2
3 December: (Cleveland), Jerome Kelly	W KO 1

1989
4 February: (Biloxi), Joe Goodman	W KO 2
10 February: (Waukesha), Anthony Jackson	W KO 1
19 February: (Monessen), Tyrone McKnight	W RSC 2
14 April: (Milwaukee), Terrence Wright	W RSC 1

24 June: (Atlantic City), Dennis Milton   Loss Pts 6
21 September: (Atlantic City), Ralph Ward   L Pts 8
14 December: (Saginaw), Willie Caldwell   W KO 1

1990
20 January: (Auburn Hills), James Williamson   W KO 1
10 March: (Bristol), Ron Martin   W RSC 1
26 April: (Atlantic City), Brinatty Maquilon   W RSC 3
12 June: (Metairie), James Fernandez   W RSC 2
21 August: (Auburn Hills), Sanderline Williams   W Pts 8
14 September (Benoit), Charles Hollis   W Pts 8
14 November: (Phoenix), José Da Silva   W RSC 3
15 December: (Pittsburgh), Danny Mitchell   W KO 1

1991
1 March: (Duluth), Ken Hulsey   W KO 1
27 July: (Norfolk), Ivory Teague   W RSC 3
13 August: (Auburn Hills), Sammy Brooks   W RSC 1
20 November: (London), John Mugabi, for the
vacant WBO middleweight title. Not defended.   W RSC 1

1992
24 February: (Auburn Hills), Lester Yarbrough   W KO 1
15 May: (Atlantic City), Carl Sullivan   W RSC 1
7 November: (Lake Tahoe), Steve Harvey   W RSC 1

1993
20 February: (Mexico City), Tyrone Moore   W RSC 2
8 May: (Las Vegas), Julian Jackson, challenging for
the WBC middleweight title.   W RSC 5
6 August: (Bayamon, Puerto Rico), Jay Bell,
WBC middleweight title defence.   W KO 1

1994
4 March: (Las Vegas), Gilbert Baptist, WBC
middleweight title defence.   W RSC 1

7 May: (Las Vegas), Julian Jackson, WBC
middleweight title defence.   W KO 1
(December, 1994, gives up the WBC title.)

1995
25 February: (London), Nigel Benn, challenging for
WBC super-middleweight title.   L KO 10

NIGEL BENN

Born: Ilford, 22 January 1964.
Height: 5ft 10in.
Last registered fighting weight: 12st.

Amateur record
1986: London and ABA middleweight champion.

Professional record
42 wins (35 stoppages), one draw, 5 losses (3 stoppages).
1988–1989: Commonwealth middleweight champion.
1990: WBO middleweight champion.
1992–1996: WBC super-middleweight champion.

Estimated career earnings: £10 million.

1987

28 January: (Croydon), Graeme Ahmed	Win RSC 2
4 March: (Basildon), Kevin Roper	W RSC 1
22 April: (Royal Albert Hall, London), Rob Nieuwenhuizen	W RSC 1
9 May: (Battersea), Winston Burnett	W RSC 4
17 June: (Royal Albert Hall), Reginald Marks	W RSC 1
1 July: (Royal Albert Hall), Leon Morris	W KO 1
9 August: (Windsor), Eddie Smith	W KO 1
16 September: (Royal Albert Hall), Winston Burnett	W RSC 3

18 October: (Windsor), Russell Barke	W RSC 1
3 November: (Bethnal Green), Ronnie Yeo	W RSC 1
24 November: (Wisbech), Ian Chantler	W KO 1
2 December: (Royal Albert Hall), Reggie Miller	W KO 7

1988

27 January: (Bethnal Green), Fermin Chirinos	W KO 2
7 February: (Stafford), Byron Price	W RSC 2
24 February: (Aberavon), Greg Taylor	W RSC 2
14 March: (Norwich), Darren Hobson	W KO 1
20 April: (Muswell Hill), Abdul Umaru Sanda, for the Commonwealth middleweight title.	W RSC 2
28 May: (Royal Albert Hall), Tim Williams	W RSC 2
26 October: (Royal Albert Hall), Anthony Logan, Commonwealth middleweight title defence.	W KO 2
10 December: (Crystal Palace), David Noel, Commonwealth middleweight title defence.	W RSC 1

1989

8 February: (Royal Albert Hall), Mike Chilambe, Commonwealth middleweight title defence.	W KO 1
28 March: (Glasgow), Mbayo Wa Mbayo	W KO 2
21 May: (Finsbury Park), Michael Watson, Commonwealth middleweight title defence.	L KO 6
20 October: (Atlantic City), Jorge Amparo	W Pts 10
1 December: (Las Vegas), Jose Quinones	W RSC 1

1990

14 January: (Atlantic City), Sanderline Williams	W Pts 10
29 April: (Atlantic City), Doug De Witt, challenging for the WBO middleweight title.	W RSC 8
10 August: (Las Vegas), Iran Barkley, WBO middleweight title defence.	W RSC 1
18 November: (Birmingham), Chris Eubank, WBO middleweight title defence.	L RSC 9

1991

3 April: (Bethnal Green), Robbie Sims	W RSC 7
3 July: (Brentwood), Kid Milo	W RSC 4
26 October: (Brentwood), Lenzie Morgan	W Pts 10
7 December: (Manchester), Hector Lezcano	W KO 3

1992

19 February: (Muswell Hill), Dan Sherry	W RSC 3
23 May: (Birmingham), Thulane Malinga	W Pts 10
3 October: (Marino), Mauro Galvano, for the WBC super-middleweight title.	W RSC 3
12 December: (Muswell Hill), Nicky Piper, WBC super-middleweight title defence.	W RSC 11

1993

6 March: (Glasgow), Mauro Galvano, WBC super-middleweight title defence.	W Pts 12
26 June: (Olympia, London), Lou Gent, WBC super-middleweight title defence.	W RSC 4
9 October: (Old Trafford, Manchester), Chris Eubank, WBC super-middleweight title defence.	Draw 12

1994

26 February: (Earls Court, London), Henry Wharton, WBC super-middleweight title defence.	W Pts 12
10 September: (Birmingham), Juan Carlos Gimenez, WBC super-middleweight title defence.	W Pts 12

1995

25 February: (London Arena), Gerald McClellan, WBC super-middleweight title defence.	W KO 10
22 July (London Arena), Vincenzo Nardiello, WBC super-middleweight title defence.	W RSC 8
2 September: (Wembley), Danny Perez, WBC super-middleweight title defence.	W RSC 7

2 March: (Newcastle), Thulane Malinga, WBC
super-middleweight title defence.   L Pts 12
6 July: (Manchester), Steve Collins, challenging for
the WBO super-middleweight title.   L RSC 4
9 November: (Manchester), Steve Collins,
challenging for the WBO super-middleweight title.   L RSC 6

ANALYSIS

Their careers ran alongside each other from the middle of 1988 to the start of 1995, nearly seven years.

Their only common opponent was Sanderline Williams.

A skilful boxer who fought the best, Williams took Benn the scheduled ten rounds in Atlantic City in January 1990, Benn's third fight in America.

That August, Williams went the full eight with McClellan at Auburn Hills, Detroit. McClellan was in the middle of a bum's tour, on his way to meeting John Mugabi in London the following year. The Williams fight was a rare, good learning experience for McClellan.

Benn had considerably more championship experience over the extra three years of his professional career, and more hard fights. He'd been in trouble, been stopped and had got up from knock-downs for spectacular wins, most notably against Anthony Logan. Defeat there would have been a setback from which he might not have recovered.

McClellan's only crises on the way up were two points losses in 1989, but they were put down to a clash of styles. He was out-tricked by solid pros, Dennis Milton and Ralph Ward.

Milton, a former national amateur light-middleweight champion, was twenty-seven at the time and had eleven wins from fourteen professional outings. He would go on to outpoint Robbie Sims (who lost to Benn) and the expatriate Liverpudlian Michael Olajide that year, then get knocked out in a round by Julian Jackson in 1991. Bernard Hopkins stopped him in four rounds in 1992 and he retired in 1995, a month before McClellan fought Benn.

Going into his fight with McClellan, Ward, from Ohio, was twenty-six, a light puncher who had been boxing for nearly three years. He'd won twelve of fifteen fights, losing on points over eight to Lindell Holmes, and over ten to Terry Norris shortly beforehand.

In a career that finished in 1998, Ward was stopped three times and scored just two early wins. Gerald seriously considered retiring after this loss, but rebuilt his career with a series of quick knockouts. Only Williams extended him during that rehabilitation.

By the time he reached London the second time, McClellan was a former world champion with a quicker knockout record than Joe Louis. Only Roy Jones Jr was thought capable of extending him.

Benn and McClellan both quit in their last fights.

And both were great fighters.